AMERICAN LITERATURE

AMERICAN LITERATURE
The New England Heritage

Edited, with an introduction, by
James Nagel and Richard Astro

GARLAND PUBLISHING, INC. ● NEW YORK & LONDON
1981

Library of Congress Cataloging in Publication Data

Main entry under title:

American literature.

   Papers presented at a conference held at North-
eastern University, May 9–10, 1980.
   Includes bibliographical references and index.
   1. American literature—New England—History
and criticism—Congresses.   I. Nagel, James.
II. Astro, Richard.   III. Northeastern University,
Boston.
PS243.A53   813'.00974   80-8517
ISBN 0-8240-9467-0

Printed on acid-free, 250-year-life paper

Manufactured in the United States of America

for
Melvin Mark

Contents

AMERICAN LITERATURE

Introduction

On May 9–10, 1980, Northeastern University sponsored a conference entitled "American Literature: The New England Heritage." At the university conference center in Weston, Massachusetts, ten speakers addressed different aspects of the rich and complex literary culture of the region, from the earliest contributions of its Puritan founders to the works of such contemporary immigrants as Bernard Malamud and Norman Mailer. The essays in this volume are, with only minor alterations, the papers presented at that conference.

A century and a half has passed since the flowering of New England began, since Ralph Waldo Emerson, Henry David Thoreau, and Nathaniel Hawthorne established Boston as the literary capital of the nation. Nearly a century has elapsed since New England's Indian Summer ended with the last works of Henry Adams and Emily Dickinson. And a half-century has passed since Van Wyck Brooks, Perry Miller, and Samuel Eliot Morison chronicled the development of the New England literary experience in their critical masterworks.

In this century, the literary center of America has shifted twice and is shifting again. It moved first to the Middle West, where, in the early part of the century, Theodore Dreiser, H. L. Mencken, Sherwood Anderson, and Carl Sandburg provided literary leadership; then to the South, where William Faulkner and Thomas Wolfe, Erskine Caldwell, Alan Tate, and John Crowe Ransom occasioned a new and vibrant literary tradition; and, most recently, to the American West, where such disparate figures as Theodore Roethke and Gary Snyder, William Stafford and Ken Kesey have helped foster the healthiest regionalism of the current age. In contrast, in New England Walden Pond has become a weekend swimming hole where local entrepreneurs charge four dollars for parking, the Old Manse is visited chiefly by "freedom trailers" en route to renew their patriotism "by the rude bridge that arched the flood," and the name of Henry Wadsworth

Longfellow is more closely identified with a Neil Diamond lyric than with the poet who sang of Hiawatha.

Yet despite the vagaries of the contemporary situation, there is no doubt that the New England literary tradition has produced the deepest and richest vein in American culture. The colonists of New England, whether out of religious fervor or artistic zeal, established what must forever be regarded as the foundation of the literary tradition of the United States. In its beginnings Anne Bradstreet, Cotton Mather, William Bradford, Edward Taylor, and others began the literary exploration of the meaning of the American experience. Later, Emerson and Thoreau, Hawthorne and Herman Melville, Louisa May Alcott, Sarah Orne Jewett, Harriet Beecher Stowe, Henry Adams, and scores of others continued this examination of the great debates between idealism and opportunity, between the spiritual New World errand and the economic materialism of Old World colonial imperialism, between the European cultural heritage and developing indigenous artistic forms, between the view of a limitless and forever expanding frontier and the more somber realities of a world of scarce resources and shrinking possibilities. The current American dialectic between those who urge restraint, a tempered idealism, and those who continue to sound the clarion of material advance, is firmly imbedded in the form and fibre of the New England heritage.

The essays in this volume define and discuss this tradition. In diverse ways they identify the New England literary tradition and explore its special historical richness, the peculiar regional genius that gave rise to a literary production unequaled in scope and depth by that of any other area in America. But more importantly, the authors of these essays present new and invigorating assessments of the nature of that production, forcing a new definition of New England letters and, as a direct result, of American literature. From a provocative demonstration of the role of humor in colonial life and art, to a new call for an appreciation of the literary expressions of the Early National Period, to a reassessment of the role of Black writers in the history of New England letters, to a sober evaluation of the contemporary novel, these essays forge a comprehensive and yet detailed discussion of the impact and continuing influence of the literature of New England.

The participants in the New England Heritage conference require little introduction to serious students of American literature. Harrison

T. Meserole is Professor of English and Chairman of the American Studies Program at Pennsylvania State University. He is also Director of the Center for Research in Textual Studies and Bibliography, from which position he serves as Bibliographer for the *American Literature* bibliography and of the *World Shakespeare Bibliography*. For nine years he served as the Bibliographer of the Modern Language Association. His books include *Seventeenth-Century American Poetry*, published in 1968 and twice reprinted; the well-known anthology *American Literature: Tradition and Innovation*, edited with Brom Weber and Walter Sutton; and *Guide to English and American Literature*, which he prepared in cooperation with F. W. Bateson. He is currently completing an edition of David Dunster's *Gospelmanna* of 1638 and working on *A Cumulated World Shakespeare Bibliography, 1958-1978* under a grant from the National Endowment for the Humanities. In " 'A Kind of Burr': Colonial New England's Heritage of Wit" he demonstrates the need for a reinterpretation of the role of humor in Colonial letters of the region, showing that wit and satire were far more pervasive in the literature of the period than has been assumed in the standard literary histories.

Lawrence Buell is a Professor of English at Oberlin College, where he has taught since receiving his Ph.D. from Cornell in 1966. He has published widely in early nineteenth-century American literature in such journals as *Texas Studies in Literature and Language, American Quarterly*, and *American Literature*. His article "Transcendental Catalogue Rhetoric: Vision Versus Form" won the 1968 Norman Foerster Prize from the Modern Language Association as the best article of the year in *American Literature*. His book *Literary Transcendentalism: Style and Vision in the American Renaissance* was nominated for a Pulitzer Prize in 1973. He is currently working on a study of the literary history of New England in the period from 1780 to 1860 under a grant from the National Endowment for the Humanities. In "The Early National Period and the New England Literary Tradition" he analyzes why this period has been long neglected in scholarship and shows why a study of this period is essential for a comprehensive understanding of the literary tradition of New England.

Joel Myerson is an Associate Professor of English at the University of South Carolina, where he has taught since receiving his

Ph.D. in English from Northwestern University in 1971. His bibliography lists eleven books, nearly all of them directly relating to Transcendentalism in New England, including a bibliography and a collection of primary materials on Brook Farm, five books on Margaret Fuller, including the recently published *Critical Essays on Margaret Fuller,* and two volumes of the *Dictionary of Literary Biography.* An ongoing project is his editorship of the distinguished annual *Studies in the American Renaissance.* His current work involves four books on Ralph Waldo Emerson: two collections of scholarly essays, a descriptive bibliography being done on an NEH grant, and an annotated secondary bibliography. His paper "Historic Notes on Life and Letters in Transcendental New England" grows directly out of this research. In it he explores Emerson's views of religion, education, government, and materialism in various aspects of Puritan culture as it had been passed down to his own generation.

Hershel Parker is H. Fletcher Brown Professor of English at the University of Delaware, where he has taught since leaving the University of Southern California in 1979. With Harrison Hayford and G. Thomas Tanselle, he has edited six volumes of Herman Melville's works for the Northwestern University Press and The Newberry Library, along with numerous other volumes of Melville's novels and short stories. His articles on American literature and textual editing have appeared in the leading journals in the field, including *American Literature, Studies in American Fiction, Proof: The Yearbook of American Bibliographical and Textual Studies,* and *Nineteenth-Century Fiction.* His books include *The Recognition of Herman Melville* (1976), *Moby-Dick as Doubloon: Essays and Extracts (1851–1970),* edited with Harrison Hayford in 1970, *Shorter Works of Hawthorne and Melville* (1972), and, with Steven Mailloux, *Checklist of Melville Reviews* (1975). He is currently finishing a collection of essays entitled *Critical Essays on Melville's Pierre* to be published by G. K. Hall. In "Melville and the Berkshires: Emotion-Laden Terrain, 'Reckless Sky-Assaulting Mood,' and En-croaching Wordsworthianism," as he proclaims in his first paragraph, he explores the effect of the Berkshires on Herman Melville in the summer of 1850, Melville's trauma of 1852, and the influence of William Wordsworth on the entire Berkshire experience.

William H. Robinson is a Professor of English at Rhode Island College, where he has taught since 1970. He received his Ph.D. from

Harvard in 1964. He has been a Visiting Scholar in Black Studies at the University of Iowa, Southern Methodist University, Boston University, and, representing Harvard University, in Italy. His lectures for the Boston Public Library, sponsored by the National Endowment for the Humanities, were published in 1977 as a book entitled *New England Black Letters.* His other books include *Early Black American Poets* (1969), *Early Black American Prose* (1970), *NOMMO: A Modern Anthology of Black African and Black American Literature* (1972), *Phillis Wheatley: In the Black American Beginnings* (1975), and *The Proceedings of the Free African Union Society of Newport, R.I. 1780–1824* (1976). He is currently at work on *A Bio-Bibliography of Phillis Wheatley* and *Critical Essays on Phillis Wheatley,* both books to be published by G. K. Hall. His essay "Earlier Black New England: The Literature of the Black I Am" provides an overview of Black literature in New England prior to the Harlem Renaissance of the 1920s, especially those works which helped to shape the moral, political, psychological, and spiritual identity of Black people in America.

Leslie Fiedler is a Professor of English at the State University of New York at Buffalo, where he has taught since 1964. He is also an Associate Fellow of Calhoun College at Yale University. He has lectured at universities all over the world and has won nearly every academic award possible, including two Fulbright Fellowships, the Christian Gauss Fellowship at Princeton, and a Guggenheim. He has published over twenty books, many of them among the best-known scholarly books in America: *An End to Innocence* (1955), *Love and Death in the American Novel* (1960), *The Last Jew in America* (1966), *The Return of the Vanishing American* (1968), and, more recently, *Freaks: Myths and Images of the Secret Self* (1978). In "New England and the Invention of the South" he explores the influence of Harriet Beecher Stowe's *Uncle Tom's Cabin* on the South, particularly on the image of the ante-bellum South, American slavery, and abolition, which, because of her novel, have become part of the national myth.

Martin Green was born in London and took a B.A. and M.A. at St. John's College, Cambridge, and studied at the University of London and the Sorbonne before receiving his Ph.D. from the University of Michigan in 1957. He taught in Turkey and France before coming to Wellesley College in 1957 and to Tufts University in 1963, where he

is now a Professor of English. He has published eleven books on a
wide range of subjects, two of which deal with New England literature
and culture: *Reappraisals: Some Commonsense Readings in American Literature* (1963) and *The Problem of Boston: Some Readings
in Cultural History* (1966). He published a novel, *The Earth Again
Redeemed,* in 1978. His research has been supported by two
Guggenheim Fellowships and by a Woodrow Wilson Center Fellowship. His essay "Literary Boston: The Change of Taste at the End of
the Century" explores the implications of the popularity of the works
of Rudyard Kipling in Boston at the end of the nineteenth century,
associating this taste with a number of other cultural phenomena of
the same period.

Since he began his academic career, Samuel French Morse has
taught at Harvard, Colby, Maine, Trinity College, Mount Holyoke,
and Northeastern University. Over the years he has received a
Fellowship from the American Council of Learned Societies and a
Fulbright Lectureship at the University of Canterbury in New
Zealand. He has lectured, and read from his verse, in New Zealand,
Australia, India, Egypt, Japan, South Korea, Bangladesh, and
Pakistan, as well as at nearly all the major universities in the United
States. He reviews regularly for the *New York Times Book Review,
Poetry* magazine, *Wisconsin Studies in Contemporary Literature,*
and other leading publications. His books include three volumes of his
own poetry (*Time of Year, The Scattered Causes,* and *The Changes*)
along with a bibliography of Wallace Stevens, the edition of two
volumes of Stevens' works, and the well-known bio-critical study
Wallace Stevens: Poetry as Life, published in 1970. Throughout
"Robert Frost: Society and Solitude" he explores the influence of
other New England poets, especially Emerson and Thoreau, on
Robert Frost's works as well as Frost's unique sense of place in his
verse.

Linda W. Wagner is a Professor of English and Associate Dean of
the College of Arts and Letters at Michigan State University, where
she has taught since 1968. In recent years she has been a Radcliffe
Institute Fellow, a Guggenheim Fellow, and the recipient of the
Distinguished Faculty Award at Michigan State. She has earned
distinction in creative writing, in administration, and in her prodigious
scholarship, which includes over twenty books. Beyond her well-
known work on Hemingway and Faulkner, her bibliography includes

two books on Denise Levertov, *Robert Frost: The Critical Heritage,* two studies of William Carlos Williams, and another entitled *E. E. Cummings: The Poet and His Critics.* The importance of "45 Mercy Street and Other Vacant Houses" is in probing the unique contributions of women poets in New England from Emily Dickinson to Anne Sexton and Sylvia Plath, contributions that deserve, and are beginning to receive, serious attention.

Melvin J. Friedman is a Professor of Comparative Literature at the University of Wisconsin—Milwaukee, where he has taught since 1966. He has served, at various points in his career, as Editor of *Wisconsin Studies in Comparative Literature* and *Comparative Literature Studies* and as Associate Editor of *Yale French Studies.* In 1976 he was at the University of Antwerp as a Fulbright Senior Lecturer. Despite his extensive scholarship in Comparative Literature, a list that contains scores of articles and ten scholarly books, he has maintained an ongoing interest in American literature, publishing on Ernest Hemingway, William Faulkner, F. Scott Fitzgerald, Henry James, among others. His interest in the American South prompted *The Added Dimension: The Art and Mind of Flannery O'Connor* (1966), *Configuration Critique de William Styron* (1967), and *William Styron* (1974). His other prime interest has been in American Jewish writers, an area of investigation that resulted in his present assessment, "Recent New England Fiction: Outsiders and Insiders."

The editors of this volume, James Nagel and Richard Astro, are both in the College of Arts and Sciences at Northeastern University. James Nagel is a Professor of English and Editor of *Studies in American Fiction.* He is also the General Editor of the G. K. Hall series *Critical Essays on American Literature.* In 1977 he was a Fulbright Professor in New Zealand and travelled world-wide on a lecture tour for the United States Information Service. Among his books are *Stephen Crane and Literary Impressionism* (1980), *Sarah Orne Jewett: A Reference Guide* (1978), *American Fiction: Historical and Critical Essays* (1977), *Critical Essays on Catch-22* (1974), and *Vision and Value* (1970). Richard Astro is Dean of the College of Arts and Sciences, a position he has held since he left the Chairmanship of the Department of English at Oregon State University in 1978. He was an American Council on Education Fellow in Academic Administration, 1974–75. His articles have appeared in

Modern Fiction Studies, Steinbeck Quarterly, Western American Literature, and elsewhere. His books include *The Fiction of Bernard Malamud* (1977) and *Hemingway in Our Time* (1974), both edited with Jackson Benson, *Edward F. Ricketts* (1976), *John Steinbeck and Edward F. Ricketts: The Shaping of a Novelist* (1973), and *Steinbeck: The Man and His Work* (1971), edited with Tetsumaro Hayashi.

The New England Heritage conference and this volume have been made possible, and greatly enriched, by the cooperation and generous assistance of scores of colleagues and friends. We would like especially to thank Professors Victor Howes, M. X. Lesser, JoAnn Gray, Samuel Bernstein, and Arthur J. Weitzman of Northeastern University, along with Richard Pearce of Wheaton College, Earl Harbert of Tulane University, Jackson Bryer of the University of Maryland, and Bernard Rosenthal of the State University of New York, Binghamton, for serving as respondents and commentators on the papers at the conference. We are deeply indebted to Mary Delay, Catherine Ezell, Alan Rooks, and David Grossblat for their efficient help in organizing and handling the logistics of the conference. Nancy Goldstein, Sarah Lowell, and Catherine Ezell also assisted in the preparation of the manuscript for publication. Gwen L. Nagel and Mary Grace Smith of Garland Publishing, Inc. were consistently gracious and professional in the production of this book. Finally, we would like to thank Melvin Mark, Provost of Northeastern University, for his confidence in us and his continuing support as we brought the New England Heritage conference and this volume to life.

James Nagel
Richard Astro

"A Kind of Burr": Colonial New England's Heritage of Wit

Harrison T. Meserole

About this time I met with an odd volume of the *Spectator.* . . . I had never before seen any of them. I bought it, read it over and over, and was much delighted with it. I thought the writing excellent, and wished, if possible to imitate it. With that view I took some of the papers, and, making short hints of the sentiment in each sentence, laid them by a few days, and then, without looking at the book, tried to complete the papers again. . . . Then I compared my *Spectator* with the original, discovered some of my faults, and corrected them . . . but I sometimes had the pleasure of fancying that in certain particulars of small import I had been lucky enough to improve the method or the language, and this encouraged me to think I might possibly in time come to be a tolerable English writer, of which I was extremely ambitious.[1]

All of us recognize, of course, one of the famous passages in American literature, written in his maturity by the man who became in his own lifetime the first internationally renowned American and whose *Autobiography* has had as much impact on life and letters on this side of the Atlantic as any document save perhaps the Bible. In the popular mind associated with Philadelphia, where he lived most of his life, Benjamin Franklin was nevertheless born in Boston, spent his

11

formative years in a Puritan household, and educated himself in his
brother's printing shop. Most important, it was in Boston that
Franklin learned to write and, within the spirit of the times, to create
the persona of Silence Dogood, whose distinctive voice has lost none
of its power after two and a half centuries.

It is understandable, therefore, and in a major sense completely
justifiable, that our best histories of American humor begin with
Franklin. Yet it does no disservice to the qualities of Franklin's
imagination to assert that some of the intonations that echo in Silence
Dogood's witty voice had been heard in earlier times in America, and
particularly in New England. At first glance this would appear
paradoxical. We have so long equated the words *New England* and
Seventeenth Century with the label *Puritan,* and this equation in turn
with the tones of solemnity heard in every major voice that speaks to
us from the time of the earliest settlements on the North Atlantic
coast, that we do not readily associate the terms *wit* and *humor* with
these voices. Yet the surface paradox begins to fade when we
remember that many of the earliest New Englanders were university-
trained and were the inheritors of a well-established Renaissance
tradition of wit, and it disappears entirely when we read widely in
what they wrote.

In keeping with the Renaissance concept of wit, in which the term
meant not only the sum of one's intellectual equipment and acumen
but also extended to accommodate various evidences of cleverness,
ingenuity, verbal facility, and high spirits, and even the assertion by
Aristotle in the *Rhetoric* that comparison is the very soul of wit, early
New England writers ranged the gamut in the kinds of wit they
composed and in the subjects they found appropriate for witty
treatment. Verbal play is in evidence from the beginning. William
Wood, for example, in 1634 published one of the most entertaining
and imaginative descriptive-promotional accounts of New England to
see print in the early years of the century. If not in every respect the
most accurate—a cure prescribed for snake bite, for example, gives
every promise of killing the patient, and the author's assertion that the
severe New England winter increases a couple's chances for procre-
ating twins must be read with appropriate forbearance—Wood's
enthusiasm for the natural beauties of the American northeast and his
keen sense of the natural wealth at hand for those who had the vision to
finance trading and exploring companies are reflected in every page of

his narrative, not only in the prose but also in the verses Wood composed to catalogue the trees and shrubs, animals (specifically the fur bearers), birds, and fish he saw or heard tales of during his two visits to America in the 1620s and 30s. The verse is doggerel, unabashedly so. And the forced rhymes and tag lines remind the sensitive reader of nothing so much as Hallmark's best. But Wood also had a sharp ear for the word or phrase that could give a dreary recital a quick awakening. The list of sea creatures begins:

> The king of waters, the Sea shouldering Whale,
> The snuffing Grampus, with the oyly Seale,
> The storme presaging Porpus, Herring-Hogge,
> Line shearing Sharke, the Catfish, and Sea Dogge. . . .

The turn comes at the close of his catalogue of shellfish:

> The luscious Lobster, with the Crabfish raw,
> The Brinish Oister, Muscle, Periwigge,
> And Tortoise sought for by the Indian Squaw,
> Which to the flats daunce many a winters Jigge,
> To dive for Cocles, and to dig for Clamms,
> Whereby her lazie husbands guts shee cramms.[2]

Wood's earthiness is matched, indeed outdone, by Nathaniel Ward, not so much in his exuberant *Simple Cobbler of Agawam,* which is perhaps the best known example of seventeenth-century American wit, as in a quatrain he composed to memorialize a particular skill possessed by John Wilson. We must recall, first, that colonial poets were particularly attracted to word games, among which the acrostic and the anagram were favorite forms. In the acrostic, lines of verse were composed so that the initial letter of the first word of each line when read vertically spelled out the name of the person to whom the poem was addressed. More intricate patterns included the variant in which the terminal letters of the final words of lines spoke a message, and the ingenious one in which letters in medial words did the same. The most elaborate example I have found in early America is by David Dunster, son of the first president of Harvard, whose manuscript *Gospelmanna* I had the pleasure of discovering four years ago and have made a preliminary report on elsewhere.[3] In this manuscript are 60 pages of verse, including a five-part acrostic composed in the shape of a cross in which two initial, two terminal, and one medial acrostic bring the "message" total to six.[4]

John Saffin of Rhode Island, whose political joustings with Governor Dudley of Massachusetts Bay became as virulent as Thomas Morton's with William Bradford over the earlier Merrymount affair, wrote perhaps the most ingenious acrostic of the time to his neighbor, Mrs. Elizabeth Hull.[5] It is at first glance a standard initial acrostic in abbreviated sonnet form—twelve lines arranged in an octave and a quatrain—replete with allusions to Phoebus, Juno, Venus, Vesta, Hymen, the Graces, Dame Nature, and assorted Nymphs to illuminate the beauties of form, face, and temperament of his subject. But the verse embodies subtleties that some external evidence quickly makes clear. Mrs. Hull was the fourth child of eight born to her parents, and she was eighteen years old on Wednesday, August 4, 1684, the fourth day of the eighth month, the day Saffin wrote the verse to her. Her name, as Saffin spelled it in the orthography of the times, contained twelve letters, with *Hull* abbreviated to *Hul* obviously to accommodate the nine-letter *Elizabeth* while maintaining the total of twelve. And if you counted the classical allusions I rehearsed above, you have noted that there are eight. Any one or two of these numerological matchings might of course be coincidental. The total of them denies coincidence and instead suggests even more strongly the fascination such stretches of ingenuity held for early New England poets.

The anagram was equally fascinating. Seventeenth-century Puritans were convinced that names were frequently revelatory of temperament or "parts" as well as of ancestry or occupation, and that the letters within names, when re-arranged to spell out other words, could illuminate the true character of the person in question. Thus it was that John Fiske of Wenham, Massachusetts, in eulogizing the renowned John Cotton in 1652 anagrammatized his name into the epigrammatic motto "O, Honie knott," made these two "new" words "honie" and "knott" thematically pervasive throughout his elegy, and in the hundred lines of the poem sought out every possible connotation and nuance of these words to construct a fugue of meanings in a coherent pattern. Thus "knott" is at once the negative, the form of a tree branch, the Gordian knot, the product of loops of cord, the incontrovertible basis for an axiom, the core of a puzzle, the road less traveled by (i.e., to grace), the component of a weave, and by metonymy, an assortment of occupations—to suggest only some of the permutations Fiske developed.

But if Fiske was the most accomplished maker of anagrams in the era, John Wilson was the most prolific and, arguably, the sharpest-tongued. Among a dissenting group whose distrust of Jesuits, Jews, Turks, Quakers, Sadduceans, Anabaptists, and other non-Puritan sects was frequently and sternly voiced, Wilson was the most combative. Claudius Gilbert, pastor of Limerick, Ireland, in 1657 published *The Libertine School'd*, a defense of the "old religion" and an attack on Quakerism, and he sent a copy to Wilson. Delighted with the book, Wilson composed the following poem and wrote it on the verso of the title page:

Claudius Gilbert

Anagram: Tis Braul I Cudgel

Tis Braul I Cudgel, Ranters, Quakers Braul,
Divels, and Jesuites, Founders of them all.
Their Brauling Questions whosoever reades
May soone perceive, These are their proper heades.
What Better Cudgels, then Gods holy word,
(For Brauls so cursed,) and the Civil sword?
By God Ordained to suppresse such evils,
Which God Abhorreth, as he doth the Devils,
Oh! Lett these blessed Cudgels knocke
     them downe.
Let Baal pleade for Baal; who are Christs,
Abhorr, oppose, Confound these Antichrists.
Yea Lett the Lord confound them, who with spight
Against his Truth maliciously Fight.[6]

Which brings us back to Nathaniel Ward, who in a neat little seven-line verse captured in a wicked image not only Wilson's propensity for verbal fireworks but also his method of composition:

We poor Agawams
are so stiff in the hams
that we cannot make Anagrams,
But Mr. John Wilson
the great Epigrammatist
Can let out an Anagram
even as he list.[7]

An equally titillating subject engaged the attention of John

Josselyn, like William Wood an early traveler to America, who recorded his impressions of the new land in *New England's Rarities Discovered*. The Indians in particular fascinated him, as they did John Eliot and Cotton Mather, who speculated that they might be descendants of one of the lost tribes of Israel. But Josselyn's eye focussed on a young Indian maiden, and in a poem that speaks clearly to us after three centuries he gave playful treatment to a tantalizing question:

> Whether White or Black be best
> Call your Senses to the quest;
> And your touch shall quickly tell
> The Black in softness doth excel,
> And in smoothness; but the Ear,
> What, can that a Colour hear?
> No, but 'tis your Black ones Wit
> That doth catch, and captive it.
> And if Slut and Fair be one,
> Sweet and Fair, there can be none:
> Nor can ought so please the tast
> As what's brown and lovely drest:
> And who'll say, that that is best
> To please one sense, displease the rest?
> Maugre then all that can be sed
> In flattery of White and Red:
> Those flatterers themselves must say
> That darkness was before the Day;
> And such perfection here appears
> It neither Wind nor Sun-shine fears.[8]

From such verbal highjinks to polemic, and its frequently used weapon, satire, is but a short step and one that early New England writers were never shy in taking. The pamphlet battle between John Cotton and Roger Williams comes immediately to mind. Cotton's views on civil and religious government in Massachusetts were attacked by Williams in *The Bloudy Tenent of Persecution* (1644), which Cotton answered in *The Bloudy Tenent Washed and Made White in the Blood of the Lamb* (1647), to which Williams replied in *The Bloudy Tenent Yet More Bloudy . . .* (1652), and so on. Equally well known is John Saffin's feud with Samuel Sewall over the manumission of Saffin's slave Adam, which occasioned not only a series of publications but also a civil proceeding that lingered almost as long in the courts as Dickens' famous Jarndyce vs. Jarndyce in *Bleak House.*

Better-natured in tone and far superior in terms of poetic accomplishment are Benjamin Tompson's mock-epic portrait of "A Fortification at Boston begun by Women" to defend Boston against the Indians during the crisis of King Philip's War, in which Tompson combined a gently satiric chuckle at the women's ineffectualness with admiration for the spirit of their endeavor,[9] and his tongue-in-cheek address to the Harvard community entitled, simply, "A Supplement":

> What meanes this silence of *Harvardine* quils
> While *Mars* triumphant thunders on our hills.
> Have pagan priests their Eloquence confin'd
> To no mans use but the mysterious mind?
> Have Pawaws charm'd that art which was so rife
> To crouch to every Don that lost his life?
> But now whole towns and Churches fire and dy
> Without the pitty of an *Elegy.* . . .[10]

It was the New England funeral elegy, of course, that moved Silence Dogood to coin the term "Kitelic Poetry" in Dogood Paper VII, published in the *New-England Courant* in June 1722, in which Franklin satirizes the form, content, tone, and poetic realization of one of the predominant types of seventeenth-century American verse. And as usual, Franklin is right on the mark. With a few notable exceptions, the early elegy is undistinguished, mechanical, and pretentious, often forced in rhyme and freighted with learned allusion. The exceptions, such as Urian Oakes' superb tribute to Thomas Shepard II, shine all the more brightly, therefore, in such a cloudy atmosphere. In his satire, Franklin is merciless. Quoting from the elegy on Mehitebell Kitel, he has Silence exclaim, "I will leave . . . Readers to judge, if ever they read any Lines, that would sooner make them *draw their Breath* and Sigh, if not shed Tears, than these following:

> Come let us mourn, for we have lost a
> Wife, a Daughter, and a Sister,
> Who has lately taken Flight, and
> Greatly we have mist her."[11]

Certainly the best known piece of Colonial American literary satire,

Franklin's "Receipt" stands in clear relationship to Anne Bradstreet's
equally well known "Author to Her Book" and provides the impetus
for what in my judgment is the wittiest example of the genre to see
print before Poe.

Embarrassed by the premature publication of *The Tenth Muse,*
Anne Bradstreet exclaimed:

> Thou ill-form'd offspring of my feeble brain,
> Who after birth did'st by my side remain,
> Till snatcht from thence by friends,
>   less wise then true
> Who thee abroad, expos'd to publick view,
> Made thee in raggs, halting to th' press to trudg,
> Where errors were not lessened (all may judg)
> At thy return my blushing was not small,
> My rambling brat (in print) should mother call,
> I cast thee by as one unfit for light,
> Thy Visage was so irksome in my sight;
> Yet being mine own, at length affection would
> Thy blemishes amend, if so I could:
> I wash'd thy face, but more defects I saw,
> And rubbing off a spot, still made a flaw.
> I stretch'd Thy joynts to make thee even feet,
> Yet still thou run'st more hobling then is meet;
> In better dress to trim thee was my mind,
> But nought save home-spun Cloth, i'th'house I find
> In this array, 'mongst Vulgars mayst thou roam
> In Criticks hands, beware thou dost not come;
> And take thy way where yet thou art not known,
> If for thy Father askt, say, thou hadst none:
> And for thy Mother, she alas is poor,
> Which caus'd her thus to send thee out of door.[12]

Antedating Franklin in recognizing the shortcomings of the
funeral elegy but equally intent on offering an appropriate tribute to a
revered teacher, Benjamin Tompson published a 76-line poem with a
typical seventeenth-century title: "The Grammarians Funeral. Or,
An ELEGY composed upon the Death of . . . the Venerable Mr.
Ezekiel Cheevers, The late and famous School-Master of *Boston* in
New-England; Who Departed this Life the *Twenty-first* of *August*
1708. Early in the Morning. In the Ninety-fourth Year of his Age."
And in equally typical seventeenth-century fashion, Tompson con-

cluded *"Sic Maestus Cecinit"* (Thus sorrowfully composed). But Tompson did not permit his sorrow at Cheever's passing to become maudlin. Instead, he begins the elegy—

> Eight Parts of Speech this Day wear
> *Mourning Gowns*
> Declin'd *Verbs, Pronouns, Participles, Nouns.*
> And not declined, *Adverbs* and *Conjunctions,*
> In *Lillies* Porch they stand to do their functions.
> With *Preposition*; but the most affection
> Was still observed in the *Interjection*—[13]

and throughout the remainder of the poem manages to work in the principal declension and conjugation patterns of Latin nouns and verbs, matters of syntax and construction, diction, problems of gender—all those details, in short, that engaged Cheever's mind as master of the Boston Latin School. A *tour de force*, admittedly, the elegy is nonetheless a witty and a memorable one.

The laurels for achievement in this sub-genre, however, belong without doubt to a late eighteenth-century man who, like Franklin, was born in Boston and later moved to Philadelphia and became one of that city's most accomplished editors, a critic of repute, and a premier essayist. Today known only to specialists in Colonial American studies, Joseph Dennie deserves a wider audience, particularly for this gem which I hope will become better known.

> Among critical writers it is a common remark, that the fashion of the times has often given a temporary reputation to performances of very little merit, and neglected those, much more deserving of applause. This circumstance renders it necessary that some person of sufficient sagacity to discover and to describe what is beautiful, and so impartial as to disregard vulgar prejudices, should guide the public taste, and raise merit from obscurity. Without arrogating to myself these qualities, I shall endeavour to introduce to the nation a work, which, though of considerable elegance, has been strangely overlooked by the generality of the world. The performance to which I allude, has never enjoyed that celebrity to which it is entitled, but it has of late fallen into disrepute, chiefly from the simplicity of its style, which, in this age of luxurious refinement, is deemed only a secondary beauty, and from its being the favourite of the young, who can relish, without being able to illustrate, its excellence. I

rejoice that it has fallen to my lot to rescue from neglect this
inimitable poem; for, whatever may be my diffidence, as I shall
pursue the manner of the most eminent critics, it is scarcely
possible to err. The fastidious reader will doubtless smile when
he is informed that the work, thus highly praised, is a poem
consisting only of four lines; but as there is no reason why a poet
should be restricted in his number of verses, as it would be a very
sad misfortune if every rhymer were obliged to write a long as
well as a bad poem; and more particularly as these verses contain
more beauties than we often find in a poem of four thousand, all
objections to its brevity should cease. I must at the same time
acknowledge that at first I doubted in what class of poetry it
should be arranged. Its extreme shortness, and its uncommon
metre, seemed to degrade it into a ballad, but its interesting
subject, its unity of plan, and, above all, its having a beginning, a
middle, and an end, decide its claim to the epic rank. I shall now
proceed; with the candour, though not with the acuteness, of a
good critic, to analyse and display its various excellences.

The opening of the poem is singularly beautiful.

Jack and Gill.

The first duty of the poet is to introduce his subject, and there is
no part of poetry more difficult. We are told by the great critic of
antiquity that we should avoid beginning 'ab ovo,' but go into the
business at once. Here our author is very happy, for instead of
telling us, as an ordinary writer would have done, who were the
ancestors of Jack and Gill, that the grandfather of Jack was a
respectable farmer, that his mother kept a tavern at the sign of the
Blue Bear; and that Gill's father was a justice of the peace, (once
of the quorum), together with a catalogue of uncles and aunts, he
introduces them to us at once in their proper persons. I cannot
help accounting it, too, as a circumstance honourable to the
genius of the poet, that he does not in his opening call upon his
muse. This is an error into which Homer and almost all the epic
writers after him have fallen; since by thus stating their cases to
the muse, and desiring her to come to their assistance, they
necessarily presupposed that she was absent, whereas there can
be no surer sign of inspiration than for a muse to come unasked.
The choice too of names is not unworthy of consideration. It
would doubtless have contributed to the splendor of the poem to
have endowed the heroes with long and soundling titles which,
by dazzling the eyes of the reader, might prevent an examination

of the work itself. These adventitious ornaments are justly disregarded by our author, who by giving us plain Jack and Gill has disdained to rely on extrinsic support. In the very choice of appellations he is however judicious. Had he, for instance, called the first character John, he might have given him more dignity, but he would not so well harmonise with his neighbour, to whom in the course of the work, it will appear, he must necessarily be joined. I know it may be said, that the contraction of names savours too much of familiarity, and the lovers of proverbs may tell us that too much familiarity breeds contempt; the learned, too, may observe, that Prince Henry somewhere exclaims, 'Here comes lean Jack, here comes bare bones,' and that the association of the two ideas detracts much from the respectability of the former. Disregarding these cavils, I cannot but remark that the lovers of abrupt openings, as in the Bard, must not deny their praise to the vivacity, with which Jack breaks in upon us.

The personages being now seen, their situation is next to be discovered. Of this we are immediately informed in the subsequent line, when we are told,

> Jack and Gill
> Went up a hill.

Here the imagery is distinct, yet the description concise. We instantly figure to ourselves the two persons travelling up an ascent, which we may accommodate to our own ideas of declivity, barrenness, rockiness, sandiness, &c. all which, as they exercise the imagination, are beauties of an high order. The reader will pardon my presumption if I here attempt to broach a new principle which no critic, with whom I am acquainted, has ever mentioned. It is this: that poetic beauties may be divided into *negative* and *positive,* the former consisting in the mere absence of fault, the latter in the presence of excellence; the first of an inferior order, but requiring considerable critical acumen to discover them, the latter of a higher rank, but obvious to the meanest capacity. To apply the principle in this case, the poet meant to inform us that two persons were going up a hill. Now the act of going up a hill, although Locke would pronounce it a very complex idea comprehending person, rising ground, trees, &c. &c. is an operation so simple as to need no description. Had the poet, therefore, told us how the two heroes went up, whether in a cart or a waggon, and entered into the thousand particulars which the subject involves they would have been tedious, because superfluous. The omission of these little incidents, and telling us simply that they went up the hill, no matter how, is a very high negative beauty. These considerations may furnish us with the means of deciding a controversy, arising from a variation in the manuscripts; some of which have *a* hill, and others *the* hill, for as the description is in no other part local, I incline to the former reading. It has, indeed, been suggested that the hill here mentioned was Parnassus, and that the two persons are two poets, who having overloaded Pegasus, the poor jaded creature was obliged to stop at the foot of the hill, whilst they ascended for water to recruit him. This interpretation, it is true, derives some countenance from the consideration that Jack and Gill were in reality, as will appear in the course of the poem, going to draw water, and that there was such a place as Hippocrene, that is a *horsepond,* at the top of the hill; but, on the whole, I think the text, as I have adopted it, to be the better reading.

Having ascertained the names and conditions of the parties, the reader becomes naturally inquisitive into their employment, and wishes to know, whether their occupation is worthy of them. This laudable curiosity is abundantly gratified in the succeeding lines; for

> Jack and Gill
> Went up a hill
> To fetch a bucket of water.

Here we behold the plan gradually unfolding, a new scene opens to our view, and the description is exceedingly beautiful. We now discover their object, which we were before left to conjecture. We see the two friends, like Pylades and Orestes, assisting and cheering each other in their labours, gaily ascending the hill, eager to arrive at the summit, and to—fill their bucket.— Here too is a new elegance. Our acute author could not but observe the necessity of machinery, which has been so much commended by critics, and admired by readers. Instead, however, of introducing a host of gods and goddesses, who might have only impeded the journey of his heroes, by the intervention of the bucket, which is, as it ought to be, simple and conducive to the progress of the poem, he has considerably improved on the ancient plan. In the management of it also he has shewn much judgment, by making the influence of the machinery and the subject reciprocal: for while the utensil carries on the heroes, it is itself carried on by them. In this part, too, we have a deficiency supplied, to wit, the knowledge of their relationship which as it would have encumbered the opening, was reserved for this place. Even now there is some uncertainty whether they were related by the ties of consanguinity; but we may rest assured they were friends, for they did join in carrying the instrument; they must, from their proximity of situation, have been amicably disposed, and if one alone carried the utensil, it exhibits an amiable assumption of the whole labour. The only objection to this opinion is an old adage, 'Bonus dux bonum facit militem,' which has been translated 'A good Jack makes a good Gill,' thereby intimating a superiority in the former. If such was the case, it seems the poet wished to shew his hero in retirement, and convince the world, that, however illustrious he might be, he did not despise manual labour. It has also been objected, (for every Homer has his Zoilus), that their employment is not sufficiently dignified for epic poetry; but, in answer to this, it must be remarked, that it was the opinion of Socrates, and many other philosophers, that beauty should be estimated by utility, and surely the purpose of the heroes must have been beneficial. They ascended the rugged mountain to draw water, and drawing water is certainly more conducive to human happiness than drawing blood, as do the boasted heroes of the Iliad, or roving on the ocean, and invading other men's property, as did the pious AEneas. Yes! they went to draw water. Interesting scene! It might have been drawn for the purpose of culinary consumption; it might have been to quench the thirst of the harmless animals who relied on them for support; it might have been to feed a sterile soil, and to revive the drooping plants, which they raised by their labours. Is not our author more judicious than Apollonius, who chooses for the heroes of his Argonautics a set of rascals, undertaking to steal a sheep skin? And, if dignity is to be considered, is not drawing water a circumstance highly cha-racteristic of antiquity? Do we not find the amiable Rebecca busy at the well—does not one of the maidens in the Odyssey delight us by her diligence in the same situation, and has not a learned Dean proved that it was quite fashionable in Pelo-ponnesus?—Let there be an end to such frivolous remarks. But the descriptive part is now finished, and the author hastens to the catastrophe. At what part of the mountain the well was situated, what was the reason of the sad misfortune, or how the prudence of Jack forsook him, we are not informed, but so, alas! it happened,

Jack fell down—

Unfortunate John! At the moment when he was nimbly, for aught
we know, going up the hill, perhaps at the moment when his toils
were to cease, and he had filled the bucket, he made an
unfortunate step, his centre of gravity, as the philosophers would
say, fell beyond his base, and he tumbled. The extent of his fall
does not however appear until the next line, as the author feared
to overwhelm us by a too immediate disclosure of his whole
misfortune. Buoyed by hope, we suppose his affliction not quite
remediless, that his fall is an accident to which the way-farers of
this life are daily liable, and we anticipate his immediate rise to
resume his labours. But how are we deceived by the heart-
rending tale, that

Jack fell down
And broke his crown—

Nothing now remains but to deplore the premature fate of the
unhappy John. The mention of the *crown* has much perplexed
the commentators. The learned Microphilus, in the 513th page
of his 'Cursory remarks' on the poem, thinks he can find in it
some allusion to the story of Alfred, who he says, is known to
have lived during his concealment in a mountainous country,
and as he watched the cakes on the fire, might have been sent to
bring water. But his acute annotator, Vandergruten, has detected
the fallacy of such a supposition, though he falls into an equal
error in remarking that Jack might have carried a crown or a half
crown in his hand, which was fractured in the fall. My learned
reader will doubtless agree with me in conjecturing that as the
crown is often used metaphorically for the head, and as that part
is, or without any disparagement to the unfortunate sufferer
might have been, the heaviest, it was really his pericranium
which sustained the damage. Having seen the fate of Jack, we are
anxious to know the lot of his companion. Alas!

And Gill came tumbling after.

Here the distress thickens on us. Unable to support the loss of his
friend, he followed him, determined to share his disaster, and
resolved, that as they had gone up together, they should not be
separated as they came down.*

---

* There is something so tenderly querimonious in the silent grief and
  devotion of Gill, something which so reminds us of the soft complaint

In the midst of our affliction, let us not, however, be unmindful of the poet's merit, which on this occasion is conspicuous. He evidently seems to have in view the excellent observation of Adam Smith, that our sympathy arises not from a view of the passion, but of the situation which excites it. Instead of unnecessary lamentation, he gives us the real state of the case; avoiding at the same time that minuteness of detail, which is so common among pathetic poets, and which by dividing a passion, and tearing it to rags, as Shakespeare says, destroys its force. Thus, when Cowley tells us, that his mistress shed tears enough to save the world if it had been on fire, we immediately think of a house on fire, ladders, engines, crowd of people, and other circumstances, which drive away every thing like feeling: when Pierre is describing the legal plunder of Jaffier's house, our attention is diverted from the misery of Belvidera to the goods and chattels of him the said Jaffier, but in the poem before us the author has just hit the dividing line between the extreme conciseness which might conceal necessary circumstances, and the prolixity of narration, which would introduce immaterial ones. So happy, indeed, is the account of Jack's destruction, that had a physician been present, and informed us of the exact place of the scull which received the hurt, whether it was the occipitis, or which of the ossa bregmatis that was fractured, or what part of the lambdoidal suture was the point of injury, we could not have a clearer idea of his misfortune. Of the bucket we are told nothing, but as it is probable that it fell with its supporters, we have a scene of misery, unequalled in the whole compass of tragic description. Imagine to ourselves Jack rapidly descending, perhaps rolling over and over down the mountain, the bucket, as the lighter, moving along, and pouring forth (if it had been filled) its liquid stream, Gill following in confusion, with a quick and circular and headlong motion; add to this the dust, which they might have collected and dispersed with the blood which must have flowed from John's head, and we will witness a catastrophe highly shocking, and feel an irresistible impulse to run for a doctor. The sound, too, charmingly 'echoes to the sense,'

---

of the hapless sister of Dido, that it might delight every classical reader:

Comitemne sororem
Sprevisti moriens? Eadem me ad fata vocasses;
Idem ambas ferro dolor, atque eadem hora tulisset.

> Jack fell down
> And broke his crown
> And Gill came tumbling after.

The quick succesion of movements is indicated by an equally rapid motion of the short syllables, and in the last line Gill rolls with a greater sprightliness and vivacity, than even the stone of Sisyphus.

Having expatiated so largely on its particular merits, let us conclude by a brief review of its most prominent beauties. The subject is the *fall of men,* a subject, high, interesting, worthy of a poet: the heroes, men who do not commit a single fault, and whose misfortunes are to be imputed, not to indiscretion, but to destiny. To the illustration of the subject, every part of the poem conduces. Attention is neither wearied by multiplicity of trivial incident, nor distracted by frequency of digression. The poet prudently clipped the wings of imagination, and repressed the extravagance of metaphorical decoration. All is simple, plain, consistent. The moral too, that part without which poetry is useless sound, has not escaped the view of the poet. When we behold two young men, who but a short moment before stood up in all the pride of health, suddenly falling down a hill how must we lament the *instability* of all things.[14]

Other aspects of wit appear, of course, in the first two centuries of New England writing. Rhetorical play, particularly the pun and such strategies as the oxymoron and understatement, is pervasive, and there are examples aplenty of riddles, apothegms, burlesques, and gravestone humor. Sarah Kemble Knight was an adept user of the comic stereotype and the amusing anecdote, and there are even instances of bawdry and of the famous three- and four-letter word Anglo-Saxon vocabulary. Benjamin Church, best known for his 1757 poem *The Choice*, while a student at Harvard was in the habit of writing "trenchant verse" in criticism of his fellow students' poetic flights. Luckless Moses Hemmenway, for example, was asked:

> Now more Detested, Vulgar and more low,
> A Fool probatur, proud, supremely so.
> Was it for you, to native Seats to rise,
> And sing of Feats between a Negroes Thighs?
> Was it Ambition not to be forgot,
> Mov'd you to sing your Race on whom begat?

And another of Church's contemporaries, possibly the Harvard tutor Henry Flynt, was described by the uninhibited Benjamin as an "ugly Monster" who sported a "matted wig of piss-burnt horse-hair made. . . ."[15]

Further evidence of the lively quality of the early New England mind exists in profusion and increases steadily as more and more texts are made available to modern students of the era. But I trust I have here already grounded my basic point: that the literary heritage of New England includes a rich dimension of wit—that special kind of burr, as Lucio put it in *Measure for Measure,* that has been bequeathed to us by our colonial forebears.

NOTES

1. Larzer Ziff, ed., *Benjamin Franklin: Autobiography; Selected Writings.* With introds. by Larzer Ziff and Dixon Wecter (New York: Holt, Rinehart, and Winston, 1969 [1948]), pp. 12–13.

2. Harrison T. Meserole, ed., *Seventeenth-Century American Poetry* (New York: Doubleday, 1968), pp. 401–02.

3. Harrison T. Meserole, "New Voices from Seventeenth-Century America," pp. 24–45 in Calvin Israel, ed., *Discoveries and Considerations: Essays on Early American Literature & Aesthetics Presented to Harold Jantz* (Albany: State Univ. of New York Press, 1976).

4. David Dunster, *Gospelmanna . . .* (1683). Bound ms., The Pennsylvania State University Libraries.

5. Meserole, *Poetry,* p. 195.

6. Meserole, *Poetry,* pp. 385–86.

7. Meserole, *Poetry,* p. 368.

8. Meserole, *Poetry,* pp. 403–04.

9. Meserole, *Poetry,* pp. 235–36.

10. Meserole, *Poetry,* p. 241.

11. Leonard W. Labaree and Whitfield J. Bell, Jr., eds., *The Papers of Benjamin Franklin.* Vol. I: *January 6, 1706 through December 31, 1734* (New Haven: Yale Univ. Press, 1959), p. 24.

12. Meserole, *Poetry,* pp. 9–10.

13. Meserole, *Poetry,* Plate I (facing p. 256).

14. *The Port Folio* (Philadelphia), 4 (14 July 1804), 217–18; (30 July 1804), 233–34. Signed "N." and ascribed to Nicholas Biddle, a member of Dennie's "circle," by Harold M. Ellis (*Joseph Dennie and His Circle*) [Austin, Texas, 1915], p. 177), this mock criticism is nonetheless of a piece with some of George Canning's parodies published in *The Microcosm* (1786–1787), two of which Dennie reprinted with acknowledgement of source in earlier issues of *The Port Folio* (see, for example, the "analysis" of "Peter Piper" in Vol. 2 [29 May 1802] and that of "The Queen of Hearts" in the same vol. [24 July 1802]).

15. Clifford K. Shipton, ed., *Sibley's Harvard Graduates,* Vol. XIII: *1751–1755* (Boston: Massachusetts Historical Society, 1965), p. 380.

The Early National Period
and the New England
Literary Tradition

Lawrence Buell

The early national period (approximately 1776–1820) is usually considered a low point in American literary history, as a time of dead ends and fitful beginnings. With some notable exceptions, literary historians, as Russel Nye once put it, have regarded the era "as a sort of blank space between the Revolution and the mature work of Irving, Bryant, and Cooper."[1] This has been especially true of the study of literature in New England, which seemed temporarily to yield precedence as a literary center to Philadelphia and New York after the decline of the elder Connecticut Wits, producing no writers before 1815 of the stature of Phillip Freneau, Washington Irving, and Charles Brockden Brown. The modern resurgence of Puritan studies has not yet extended to the field of post-colonial New England literature despite a recent flurry of interest in the wake of the Bicentennial. During the 1970s, according to the *PMLA* bibliographies, more than twice as many articles and books were devoted to Puritan era figures as to the considerably greater number of New England writers who flourished between 1776 and 1820. The latter group received less critical attention during the entire decade than did Hawthorne and Melville in 1978 alone.

The most obvious reason for the neglect is that the period produced no universally recognized literary classics unless we count

Franklin's *Autobiography*, the work of a New England expatriate
begun before our *terminus a quo* and exclusively concerned with pre-
Revolutionary events. Nor are there more than a handful of recognized near classics, works like Royall Tyler's *The Contrast*, which
helped to form the stereotype of the stage Yankee, and John
Trumbull's *McFingal*, the best of the Revolutionary satires, both
sprightly but for the most part derivative. The financial failure of
Samuel Goodrich's elegant two-volume edition of Trumbull's works
in 1820 suggests how quickly even much of the better early national
period literature was forgotten by the next generation of New
Englanders. Emerson's statement that "from 1790 to 1820 there was
not a book, a speech, a conversation, or a thought, in the State" of
Massachusetts has been quoted, generally with approval, by every
subsequent generation of literary critics. The result of this and similar
pronouncements was, in time, to give rise to what Lewis Simpson has
called the "myth of New England's intellectual lapse" between the
high plateau of Puritan and Revolutionary achievement and the so-
called New England "Renaissance" of the 1830s and after.[2]
    This myth is not entirely without basis. It would have been
accepted even by many early national period intellectuals, who by
1800 were acutely conscious of having begun the 1770s with a wave
of prophetic optimism about America's future literary greatness that
the next decades had failed to bear out. The myth has the further value
of inhibiting over-eager scholars from claiming more for the literature
of the period than the facts warrant. Yet the myth is clearly also an
exaggeration arising from at least two ideological biases that have
caused literary scholars to dwell upon the Puritan and Romantic eras
at the expense of the early national period.
    First, the American literary tradition is normally seen as a
romantic tradition, whereas the literature of the early national period
is markedly Neoclassical in orientation and therefore (from the
Romanticist perspective) epiphenomenal. The problem with this view
is not so much its major premise as the deduction therefrom. The
ideology of Romanticism was admittedly more adaptable to new
world conditions than the Neoclassical ideology it superseded.[3] For
one thing, Romanticism encouraged literary autonomy as opposed to
acceptance of European literary modes and therefore provided more
of an incentive to cultural independence. Furthermore, by placing a
high value on nature and spontaneity (as opposed to the civilized,

sophisticated, urban virtues and pleasures), Romanticism converted America's underdevelopment into a national treasure and lent support to the American penchant for contrasting new world rustic simplicity and vast natural resources with old world crowdedness and decadence. In the third place, Romanticism valued individuality of style, the development of an individual voice as opposed to adherence to established standards of taste, and therefore appealed to American anti-authoritarianism. Likewise, Romanticism placed a high value upon depiction of the isolated individual consciousness, as opposed to mundane social interaction, and as a result it was able to draw more than Neoclassicism had done upon the depths of New England religious experience, the intense probing into the soul's depths that characterized Puritan and post-Puritan piety well into the nineteenth century. For this and other reasons, American literary historians have with some justice become accustomed in recent years to envisioning a kind of intellectual expressway between Puritanism and Romanticism, along which New England Neoclassicism appears mainly as a kind of "negative" phase (to use Emerson's favorite epithet for Unitarianism) in the softening of the Reformation rigor that was implanted in the 1600s and flowered into art 200 years later.[4]

The trouble with this paradigm is that it artificially narrows our vision of the New England literary canon. A book like *Walden* is elevated to classic status not merely because it is an excellent (albeit sometimes labored) piece of writing but also because it strongly reflects the Romantic values just mentioned and their Puritan antecedents. A work like *Female Quixoticism* (1801), Tabitha Tenney's once popular but now forgotten rendition of the theme of the romance-mad young woman in an American context, is a clever, worthwhile novel that may never receive its due because it is *Walden*'s aesthetic opposite. It is quite frankly not a work of original genius but an ingenious adaptation of plot motifs worked out in European fiction. It delves into its heroine's consciousness only to demonstrate how far she is out of line with common sense and socially functional behavior; it stresses the importance of conforming to accepted standards of good taste; and it tends to identify the state of nature with the state of stupidity. Though unquestionably less impressive than *Walden, Female Quixoticism* certainly deserves more than a microprint edition from Lost Cause Press. In addition to being witty and amusing, it is historically significant as a feminist

document (inculcating self-reliance and survival skills through a
counter-example), as a transitional work in the development of
"woman's fiction" (to use Nina Baym's term),[5] and as an exercise in
adapting European models to the American scene. As things stand,
Tenney is a victim of anti-Neoclassical bias.

The same bias has skewed our vision of better-known writers. If
one assumes that Romanticism is *the* American literary mainstream,
one will inevitably be tempted to exaggerate its foreshadowings in
early national period literature. Thus discussions of Timothy Dwight's
poetry customarily identify his *Greenfield Hill* (a rather insipid
pastoral about the parish where he spent his ministry) as his best
poem, at least partially because it foreshadows the personal, concrete,
nature-imagey traits of Romantic writing—and, at the opposite
extreme, to minimize the virtues of what is really by far his best poem,
The Triumph of Infidelity (a satire against the heresy of Universalism
as a pandora's box leading to moral anarchy), at least partially
because that poem looks "backward" both intellectually, to hard-line
Calvinism, and stylistically, to the manner of the Tory satirists,
Dryden, Pope, and Swift.[6] Along with several other Federalist era
poems that modern critics do not like, *The Triumph of Infidelity*
draws upon the tactics of Pope's last and bitterest major poem, *The
Dunciad*, which ends with the vision of dullness and stupidity
triumphing over the forces of civilization and order. Dwight applies
this formula to the subject of religious and moral order; other
Federalist poets, like Thomas G. Fessenden (*Democracy Unveiled*)
and the authors of *The Anarchiad*, apply it to the political order. In
each case one imagines the picture of an embattled gentleman of the
"tie-wig school" (as Parrington liked to call it) fighting innovation
with his last gasp.

The second major ideological factor inhibiting appreciation of
early national period literature in New England is antifederalist
bias. Federalism is widely pictured, by social and literary historians
alike, as an ideology that did great things for a few years (constitutional ratification and the first steps of nation building) but then
degenerated into a futile, bigoted reaction against the tide of democ-
ratization under Jefferson and Jackson. In light of present-day
American values, admittedly the Federalist philosophy that the
nation should be governed according to the best judgment of its
reputable, propertied, leading citizens, rather than by the will of the

great disreputable mass, does not seem very appealing. The fact that the great majority of noted New England literati of the early national period (including all of Joseph Dennie's circle and all of the Connecticut Wits except Joel Barlow) were outspoken Federalists who often used literature as a vehicle for political agitation increases one's reluctance to accept New England writing of the period as an authentic expression of the American mind. Works like Dwight's *Triumph*, which ridicules folk-hero and freethinker Ethan Allen as "the great Clodhopping oracle of man"; or like Tyler's *The Contrast*, which seems to present priggish Col. Manly as a model and make fun of the true-blue Yankee Jonathan; or like *McFingal*, which seems at times to satirize the Patriots as much as the Loyalists—such works do not seem fully Americanized, despite their protestations to the contrary. They seem to use satire partly as a means of preserving old-world class distinctions and standards of decorum. Their dependence upon Pope, Sheridan, and Butler as literary models reinforces this impression.

The sense of literary Federalism as un-American is further reinforced by scholarship on the antebellum period. Students of the New England Renaissance are no longer as crude as Parrington in dividing the *dramatis personae* into progressives and reactionaries, but they still tend to associate the period's dynamic elements with Jeffersonian traditions like agrarianism, broadening of the franchise, and territorial expansion. To the extent that the Emersonian doctrine of self-reliance looks forward to Whitman's deification of everyman, it is seen as a liberating, or at least as an interesting, conception. To the extent that it is qualified by Emerson's lingering distrust of the herd, it is deplored as a throwback to Federalist elitism.[7]

The sins of Federalism and of Neoclassicism are interrelated. Although the linkage is arbitrary in the sense that Neoclassicism is equally characteristic of Jeffersonian writing, the association is valid in the sense that Neoclassicism reflected Federalist values more closely than Jeffersonian values. Federalism and Neoclassicism both connote respect for tradition, distrust of social change, maintenance of time-tested cultural standards, and commitment to learned rather than popular modes of expression—none of which are commonly thought of as belonging to American literature at its most typical. Given the axiom that the great turning point in American poetry came when Whitman, "one of the roughs," liberated the genre from the shackles of polite verse, we understandably find it hard to see how fastidious heroic couplets denouncing the turbulent lower classes belong in the American canon, no matter how crisp and incisive those couplets may be.

So much for the causes of neglect. What, then, can be said on behalf of studying the likes of Joseph Dennie, Thomas Green Fessenden, and Robert Treat Paine more closely? I shall present five arguments, in what I take to be ascending order of importance.

The first is the challenge of trying fully to recapture the spirit of literary pioneering that characterized the post-Revolutionary era. To some tastes, if not to all, there is something exciting about a time of beginnings, when we see the proliferation of semi-organized, often faltering attempts to raise the level of the arts in America to a plane of respectability and at the same time a casting about in all directions to discover what the new American voice should be. The splendid amateurism of an age when a future United States President (John Quincy Adams) could, along the way, be a poet, a translator, and the nation's first professor of rhetoric; when professionals in all fields were drawn not only to patronize but to participate in the literary scene; when any person of literary talent could legitimately feel that the territory was wide open, that he or she might become the first great American writer—this ambiance has its appeal as well as its crudity and is unique to the period. We shall never see such times again.

In the second place, New England literature of the early national period was considerably more prolific than has been realized. Even though the great boom in indigenous writing came after 1815, during the previous 40 years there was a steady increase in the number of New England literary works.[8] Those to whom the period evokes only the memory of the major Connecticut Wits and a few other scattered names like Dennie's will be surprised to learn how many New England literati flourished during the era. As a rough means of separating complete nonentities from figures of at least minimal significance, let us limit our attention to writers who meet the following criteria: they must have grown up primarily in New England, or resided there half their working lives; they must have reached literary maturity between 1776 and 1820; they must have published at least one work of a primarily literary nature; and they must have been included either in the *Dictionary of American Biography*, *Notable American Women*, or in the most important antebellum compendium of American literary biography, Evert and George Duyckinck's *Cycolpaedia of American Literaure* (1856). These criteria rule in some trivial pamphleteers, but they also rule out some figures of genuine literary import, like the diarist William Bentley of Salem, the Monthly Anthologist Joseph Stevens Buckminster, and the preromantic poet Thomas Odiorne. So the criteria are on the whole pretty rigorous. At least 62 writers (listed in the Appendix) meet them. Despite the supposed literary eclipse of New England by the middle colonies during the early national period, this rate of productivity was probably significantly higher than for the country as a whole during the same period. Here is a rough means of comparison. Of the people listed in the *DAB* index under the heading of "Authors" born between 1740 and 1799, 53% were native New Englanders, whereas the mean percentage of New Englanders in the total American white population during the same six decades was only 35.7%.[9] For the category "Poets," the gap is even more striking: 64% of the listed American poets born during the six decades in question were New England natives. Only in one genre did New England underproduce relative to its share of the white population: drama. It should be added that at least seven of the 62 writers left New England permanently or for long sojourns in the hope of finding better literary or artistic opportunities elsewhere, and that these included some of the best talent: Bryant, Dennie, Allston, and Halleck. But the rate of expatriation was no greater than for the New England Renaissance period.

All 62 of the writers produced at least one fictive work except Joseph Dennie, who was exclusively a literary essayist; 24 of the 62 published one literary book or pamphlet; 10 published two; and the rest (28) three or more. I have no idea how this breakdown compares with that of other periods, but it shows that a majority of the 62 writers were "repeaters." Nine of the 25 one-book writers, incidentally, published collections of verse or prose that had been written over a period of years.

Statistics like these, of course, show output rather than quality. In themselves they do not refute the charge of literary worthlessness. Yet without seeking to claim that New England produced any unappreciated masterpieces between 1776 and 1820 of the stature of *Walden* or *The Scarlet Letter*, I would argue, in the third place, that the period contains more neglected works of literary interest, proportionally speaking, than any era in American literature before 1900. This assertion naturally cannot be substantiated without going into explications far too lengthy for such an essay as this. As a partial substitute, I have distributed at this symposium and shall gladly furnish on request a selected bibliography of works that I believe would repay more critical study than they have so far received— deliberately excluding the best-known works of the period, like Barlow's *Columbiad*, even though in some cases they too may not have received their just due.

The two most decisive arguments on behalf of the importance of early national period New England literature, however, seem to me much more easily demonstrable. Both have to do with the significance of that literature for American intellectual and literary history as a whole. The first of these two arguments would be that New England Neoclassicism cannot simply be written off as a superficial imported fashion indicative of American cultural immaturity but should be understood as genuinely adaptive to the needs of late eighteenth- and early nineteenth-century American artists and audiences. This is obviously the case with Neoclassicism in American architecture and political thought, and I believe that the situation in the literary sphere is much the same. William Hedges, Lewis Simpson, and other scholars have in fact already shown, for example, that the formality and elevation of Neoclassical style was an authentic expression of the Federalist literati's fear of anarchy, a sign of their need to impose decorum and restraint, of their desire to legitimate the new republic by grounding it on the precedents of Greece and Rome, and of their conservatively but genuinely patriotic goal for American literary self-realization—namely the ideal of a native literary establishment that would take its place in an international republic of letters, drawing upon a common reservoir of tradition and expertise, rivalling Europe on its own ground.[10] The same point is implied by Richard Bushman's recent study of colonial satire.[11] Satire, Bushman shows, did not flourish in New England until the mid-eighteenth century, with the rise of social and political factionalism. By then Butler, Dryden, Pope, Gay, and Swift were dead, well known, and even to some extent imitated, but the vogues of *Hudibras* and *The Dunciad* did not really begin until the native conditions were right for them.

As a further example, showing the fruitfulness of the theory of selective borrowing even on the humblest levels of inspiration, consider the *Miscellaneous Poems* of Jonathan Mitchel Sewall (1801). Sewall's book contains a number of items that seem merely manneristic parrotings of Neoclassical frippery, such as his address "To a Lady Who Fainted on Attempting to Smoke for the Toothache." Yet Sewall often gives his models characteristically New England twists. For example, his poem "On the Gloomy Prospects of 1776" starts with lines that seem straight out of Pope's *Essay on Man*:

> Canst thou, by searching, the Omniscient find?
> Or to perfection scan th' eternal mind?

Yet Sewall uses this opener as a springboard for a characteristic post-Puritan vision of God chastising his sinful people with the scourge of the redcoats, but upon their repentance purging them from America and ushering in "thy millennium with transcendant bliss." The subtitle says "Written with allusion to part of the 11th chapter of Job." This hint is important. The resignation and acceptance of righteous affliction that Job's story supposedly teaches is a common denominator both of the jeremiad tradition upon which Sewall draws for his theme and of Pope's poem, which supplies the literary voice. Although we normally suppose, and with justice, that the sons of the Puritans thought rather differently from the deist Catholic Pope, clearly Pope's rhetoric has helped Sewall give expression to his very un-Augustan jeremiad. What we have here and in many other such cases is a borrowing in the literary realm comparable to the sort of borrowing in the political sphere that led American and British Whigs to draw very divergent inferences from the same body of reading matter and the same constitutional heritage.

But even the argument that Federalist-style Neoclassicism was an authentic vehicle for the spirit of the age does not prove that it led to anything other than a *cul-de-sac* so far as the development of American literary history as a whole is concerned. Thus a recent essay by Robert Arner, after a very fine account of how the heroic couplet expresses the sensibility of the Connecticut Wits, comes to the bleak conclusion that

> American poetry has gone its way almost as though the Wits had never existed, had never written a line. We come back in the end to Emerson, who pioneered on the frontiers of fact and symbol,

testing and expanding the limitations of language, meter, and
meaning in a way that exposes the narrowness of the couplet
even if the Wits had been more often adept at its use.[12]

In short we revert to the familiar sequence of Edwards to Emerson
and beyond as the backbone of New England literary history, with the
Federalist literati swept back into the dustbin again after a brief airing.
In order to arouse any real enthusiasm for studying them, we have to
be able to demonstrate lines of continuity between them and
subsequent New England literary history.

This brings me to my final and most significant point. Such
continuities I believe to exist, of such number and importance as to
make a solid understanding of Federalist writing indispensable to the
New England Renaissance specialist, even if one never develops a
relish for Trumbull's hudibrastics or Dwight's invective and bombast.

The first and most familiar, however, I shall pass over quickly: i.e.,
the presence of preromantic elements in early national period
literature, as in Dwight's *Greenfield Hill*. These elements certainly
exist, perhaps in greater measure than in British literature before
Wordsworth, but their presence is too well known and too often
overstated to warrant amplification here. Americanists tend to forget,
for instance, that "preromantic" loco-descriptive poetry like Dwight's
is actually as much a Neoclassical phenomenon as a reaction against
same: the first such poem in British literature, John Denham's
Cooper's Hill (1642), is also conventionally regarded as the first
instance of the true heroic couplet in English. Furthermore, to value
Neoclassical era works for their romantic anticipations is really to
deny the period's primary aesthetic values. I turn, then, to other
continuities.

One of the most important of these has to do with the New
England Federalists' self-appointed role as arbiters of virtue and
taste. The ethos of Neoclassicism encouraged the Federalist writers'
predisposition to assume a posture of moral monitorship intermediate and transitional between that of the Puritan divines and that
of the Transcendentalists and subsequent American poet-prophets.
The Neoclassical didacticism of Addison, Pope, and Johnson blended
with the heritage of Puritan didacticism to create compounds like the
Sewall poem mentioned above and, in general, to assist Federalist
literati to conceptualize their role as lawgivers to their fellow-citizens

in a way that sets the stage for the characteristic opposition we later find between the alienated or isolated writer and the society he/she prophetically indicts and instructs. In the Federalist literati's handling of their moral monitor's role, we find, as the period unfolds, the first stages of the characteristic tension running throughout American history between middle-class society and the writer who stands in loyal or not-so-loyal opposition as its self-appointed prophet or critic. Under Federalism, the intellectual and political leadership of New England (and in America as a whole) was fused to a degree that intellectuals have been trying to recapture ever since. As their party lost its hold, the Federalist writers became the first group of alienated American intellectuals. The first really profound statement of the plight of the artist in a republic came not from Cooper or Poe or Emerson or Hawthorne but from Fisher Ames, who declared (ca. 1800) that "it is the very spirit of democracy . . . to proscribe the aristocracy of talents."[13] Our distaste for Ames's patrician arrogance should not keep us from appreciating how shrewdly he anticipates DeTocqueville and Richard Hofstadter on the subject of American anti-intellectualism, and how the Federalist literati's growing sense of themselves as an endangered species in a perpetual war against bigots, clods, philistines, and ninnies anticipates writers like Thoreau and Dickinson.

Linda Kerber, in her excellent book on Federalism, refers to a Federalist-abolitionist "continuum" in which "the political abolitionism of an earlier generation" (which she sees as a ploy to advance sectional interests) "was transformed into a humanitarian abolitionism by sons who took their fathers at their word."[14] She cites examples like Josiah and Edmund Quincy, John and Wendell Phillips, and the surrogate father-son relation of Federalist Rufus King and William Lloyd Garrison. Extending Kerber, I would suggest that we think of a more general continuum linking Federalist intellectuals with the Transcendentalists and all other New England romantic reformers who pictured themselves as commissioned to resist the tyranny of the majority and to raise the communal consciousness to a higher level of culture and moral awareness. Listen to how Thoreau's speech on John Brown's raid echoes Fisher Ames's remarks on the Jeffersonian revolution:

Thoreau: We talk about a *representative* government; but what a
monster of a government is that where the noblest faculties
of the mind, and the *whole* heart, are not *represented*. A
semi-human tiger or ox, stalking over the earth, with its
heart taken out and the top of its brain shot away. Heroes
have fought well on their stumps when their legs were shot
off, but I never heard of any good done by such a
government as that.[15]

Ames: We see ourselves in the full exercise of the forms of
election, when the substance is gone. We have some
members in Congress with a faithful meanness to represent our servility, and others to represent our nullity in the
union; but our vote and influence avail no more, than that
of the Isle of Man in the politics of Great Britain. If, then,
we have not survived our political liberty, we have lived
long enough to see the pillars of its security crumble to
powder.[16]

We hear some similar notes in these two passages: righteous
sermonizing in the jeremiad vein; a caustic, mordant gallows humor,
reflecting a tendency to view life in terms of extreme outcomes; a
sense of belonging to a select vanishing few that are charged to awaken
their countrymen from sleep; and above all a vision of the stark
discrepancy between the pleasing forms of republican government
and the actual perversion of those forms. Both passages also,
incidentally, invoke this picture as a way of combatting the supposed
domination of New England by southern interests. That is another
way in which Federalist culture in New England can be seen as
anticipating the next age: it became, especially after 1800, the first of
many substantial cases of cultural regionalism in America.

The resemblances between Ames and Thoreau make increasing
sense when we realize that the activist literati in antebellum New
England were not mostly Jacksonian Democrats, not lineal Jeffersonians, but mostly associated with the Whigs, who were the descendants
of Federalism as the party of the region's "natural aristocracy." The
New England writers who became vocal about slavery and other
public issues during the 1840s and 1850s—Emerson, Thoreau,
Lowell, Longfellow, Whittier, and Stowe—were, like Charles Sumner,
the politician they most admired, generally cool or hostile to Jackson
in the 1830s and members or fellow travelers of the reformist branch

of the Whig Party, the so-called "Conscience" Whigs. The fathers or grandfathers of the majority of them had been prominent Federalists. Federalist hauteur could also, of course, lead in due time to the Unitarian establishment Emerson attacked, to conservative Whiggery, to Brahminism, to campaigns for restrictive immigration laws. But the presence of this conservative legacy by no means negates the argument concerning Federalism's radical offshoots; on the contrary, knowing that both stem from a common source should help us better to understand such other nineteenth-century developments as the increasing rapprochement between the Concord Transcendentalists and the Boston-Cambridge literary set and the very uneasy relationship between both groups and figures like Walt Whitman and Mark Twain.

One of the chief literary weapons of the alienated radical or reactionary is satire. Satire was of course one of the hallmarks of Neoclassical writing, both in Britain and America.[17] Satire is normally not considered a core characteristic of Romanticism, and yet if we look more closely at American literature we see that this generalization does not hold. Satire is actually quite prevalent in all the major American romantics except Whitman. A number—Cooper, Emerson, Thoreau, Dickinson, and Melville—became more satiric as their careers wore on. Think for a moment of antebellum New England literature as centering around the following texts: Emerson's "New England Reformers" and "Historic Notes of Life and Letters in New England"; Thoreau's "Economy," "Civil Disobedience," "Slavery in Massachusetts," and "Life Without Principle"; Dickinson's "What Soft—Cerubic Creatures—/ These Gentlewomen are—" and "The Bible is an antique Volume—/ Written by faded Men"; Whittier's "Ichabod"; Lowell's *Fable for Critics* and *The Biglow Papers*; Hawthorne's *The Blithedale Romance*; and Holmes's *Elsie Venner*. Focusing on these as a group, we become much more aware of the continuity of New England satire on American shallowness, materialism, and provincialism between the early national and romantic periods.

To pursue a specific example, the basis of Dwight's critique in that great neglected diatribe *The Triumph of Infidelity* is much the same as that of Melville's long-unappreciated *The Confidence-Man*. Both works satirize the fallacy of trusting naively in a benign view of providence and human nature. Satan, or the Satanic principle, is shown in Dwight and suggested in Melville to be the source of these errors. In Dwight's case, the immediate target is Universalism, the doctrine that all men will finally be saved. This doctrine Dwight regards not only as false but as pernicious, as encouraging sin and the speedy destruction of humanity except for the faithful remnant. Dwight's opposition to Charles Chauncy, whose treatise on universal salvation seems to have inspired the poem, prefigures the tension between Transcendentalist optimism and the reaction thereto by Hawthorne, Dickinson, and Melville. Dwight's and Melville's satires are particularly alike in the combination of grim insistence and ironic detachment with which they erode the sugary surface of American optimism. Undoubtedly part of the reason Dwight is ignored is that he cast his critique in old-fashioned heroic couplets.

Such stylistic preferences have of course given Neoclassical literature the reputation of specious artificiality—in its verse forms, its elegance of language, its tendency to drag in a plethora of allusion. All this is a far cry from the greater pointedness of Thoreau and Dickinson, not to mention the vernacular of Seba Smith, Mary Wilkins Freeman, Rose Terry Cooke, and Rowland Robinson, in whose works we trace the unfolding of a distinctively regional idiom. At the same time, we must remember that it was during the Neoclassical era that New England manners and colloquial speech first became taken seriously by American writers. In English poetry the first large-scale attention to everyday, mundane trivia comes in those highly polished, elegant satires of the age of Dryden and Pope. Likewise, in New England writing, the best early sketches of provincial life and Yankee dialect are drawn in a humorous, patronizing context. Dwight's Ethan Allen, the great clodhopping oracle who "bustled, bruised and swore" in Satan's cause is a Constance Rourkian ring-tailed roarer Yankee folk hero not yet taken seriously. Tyler's Jonathan is the rustic Yankee yeoman not yet sentimentalized. The credit for creating these stereotypes must go at least partly to the Federalist gentry.

A particularly instructive example is Yale-educated Federalist lawyer St. John Honeywood's parody of Republican Vermont Congressman Matthew Lyon, known to Jeffersonians as a martyr of the Sedition Act but to Federalists primarily as "spitting Mat," the man who spat in the face of fellow-Congressman Roger Griswold of Connecticut on the floor of the House. Here are excerpts from

Honeywood's imaginary congressional speech by Lyon, probably
supposed to be sung to the tune of Yankee Doodle:

> I'm rugged Mat, the democrat,
>   Berate me as you please, Sir;
> True Paddy Whack ne'er turned his back,
>   Or bow'd his head to Caesar.
> *Horum, scorum, rendum, roarum,*
>   *Spittam, spattam, squirto;*
> *Tag, rag, derry, merry, raw head and bloody*
>   *bones,*
>   *Sing langolee, nobody's hurt, O!*
>
> . . . .
>
> My dam, Sir, was a buxom lass,
>   Her milk was rich and good, Sir;
> No cow that's fed on clover grass
>   Can boast of purer blood, Sir. (Refrain)
>
> My sire he was a strapping buck
>   As ever girl sat eye on;
> What wonder then they had the luck
>   To bring the world a LYON! (Refrain)[18]

On one level, this is a distinctly "elitist" poem—almost a quint-
essential example of Federalism's least attractive prejudices: dislike
of non-Anglo-Saxons, the lower classes, and miscellaneous breaches
of etiquette which, for Honeywood, lowers a fellow like Lyon to the
level his name implies—an animal. Yet on the other hand, the poem is
very close to the roots of popular literary consciousness in its ballad
form, its use of the folk-hero's heroic boast, and its mimicry of the
plain talk and assertive swagger of the man of the people. Honeywood
walks a very thin line between patrician arrogance and rough-and-
tumble horseplay and in the process shows a nearness of the
vernacular spirit that later American writers immerse themselves in
more thoroughly. Conversely we must recognize that the sense of
looking at common life from the outside also continues to persist: in
the genre sketches of Hawthorne and Lowell and even in the local
colorists we continue to get the impression of crude specimens of
bumpkinism handled condescendingly, of the washed depicting the
unwashed. The class-consciousness of the Federalist writers must be
regarded as still another legacy to New England literature.

To pursue the subject of Neoclassical "artificiality" one step further, we discover affinities with the next age even at the point we least expect them, namely the closed couplet itself, the most characteristic of Neoclassical prosodic forms. Of course we instinctively oppose the closed couplet to the more open, fluid style of Emersonian prose, as in the quotation from Robert Arner. Yet I have come to think that this may be a false dichotomy. Actually couplet verse and Transcendentalist rhetoric have at least two important traits in common: both are atomistic methods of construction that put a great premium on the individual detached saying or image, and both for this reason invite a comparatively cerebral, intellectualized reaction whatever their emotional freight. Benjamin Spencer once remarked that the early national period "regarded the incisive generalization as inherently poetic."[19] True enough. Orators loved gems like the following tribute to General Warren: "Like Harrington he wrote,—like Cicero he spoke,—like Hampden he lived,—and like Wolfe he died."[20] In such aperçu, and in the similar style of the closed couplets, we see an anticipation of the effect that Emerson and Thoreau sought in their expository prose. Both types of style, the Transcendentalist and the Federalist, show a fondness for immediate rhetorical effects as opposed to sustained and tightly knit literary wholes and at the same time a respect for learning and intellectual subtlety. The showy classicism of the Federalist literati, with their frequent displays of allusion and penchant for unnecessary footnotes, dependent for the most part on superficial college syllabi and desultory reading, looks backward to Cotton Mather's grab bag pedantry and anecdotalism and looks forward to Emerson's syncretistic interweavings of odd bits of learning from every source imaginable, likewise dependent upon superficial college syllabi and desultory reading. In each case, triumph by aphorism, by appeal to common sense axioms, and by virtuoso command of book-learning that is nevertheless reasonably accessible to the educated layperson are all important rhetorical strategies.[21]

These rhetorical strategies are, of course, predictable in a milieu where literary people feel impelled by personal preference and social pressure to assume the role of teachers-at-large and are afflicted with guilt or a sense of themselves as frivolous when, like Hawthorne, they feel uncomfortable with that role. This sense of the public mission of the serious literary artist originates in Puritan New England and continues very strongly throughout both the early national and antebellum periods, though it weakens somewhat by the mid-nineteenth century. To some extent, it underlies all the continuities described above. A final expression of it worth mentioning here is what might loosely be called apocalypticism. Early national period literature, as recent scholars have pointed out, likes to dwell on the opposite possibilities of millennial or utopian fulfillment and (at the opposite extreme) of total destruction through holocaust or divine wrath.[22] New England writing is particularly rife with such images: Barlow's *Columbiad* gives the optimistic, utopian scenario; *The Anarchiad* the tragic, dystopian outcome. Both possibilities derive from the implicit doubleness of the jeremiad tradition, which, as the disagreement between Perry Miller and Sacvan Bercovitch has proven, holds forth the prospects both of ultimate fulfillment and ultimate doom for the New English Israel.[23] The epics and mock-epics of the Connecticut Wits illustrate a secularization of the jeremiad in the literary sphere parallel to the process of secularization in the political sphere that began in the mid-eighteenth century when the literal United States became identified with the ideal, sacred goal envisioned by the Puritan divines. As such the Connecticut Wits stand at the head of a dual tradition that persists throughout American secular literature, exemplified on the one side by Emerson, Whitman, Edward Bellamy, and Hart Crane, and on the other side by Cooper (in *The Crater*), Mark Twain, Nathanael West, Allen Ginsberg, and Imamu Baraka (in his *System of Dante's Hell*). For present purposes it should not be necessary to say more about this dual tradition except that the American imagination seems to be addicted to envisioning ultimate states of social perfection or annihilation and that the Federalist period, when both possibilities may have seemed more imminent than they ever have since, marks a crucial stage in the unfolding of this tradition.

Such are some of the reasons why a lover of New England romanticism like myself began venturing backward in time, eventually to become at least mildly addicted to the forgotten figures of the Federalist era—without, let me add, abandoning my first love. In this short essay, I cannot hope to have converted the skeptical reader to my own state of enthusiasm, but I do hope at least to have begun to show why a knowledge of the early national period is more essential to a full understanding of the New England literary tradition than the current state of research, university syllabi, and omnibus anthologies imply.

Appendix

Below are listed the 62 New England literati of the early national period identified as "significant" by criteria described in this essay, together with an indication of the most recent of the three targeted reference works in which their biographies appear: the *Dictionary of American Biography* (*DAB*), *Notable American Women* (*NAW*),* and the Duyckincks' *Cyclopaedia of American Literature* (*CAL*).

John Quincy Adams (*DAB*)
Paul Allen (*DAB*)
Washington Allston (*DAB*)
Richard Alsop (*DAB*)
Josias Lyndon Arnold (*CAL*)
Joel Barlow (*DAB*)
Joseph Bartlett (*DAB*)
Jeremy Belknap (*DAB*)
Jacob Bigelow (*DAB*)
William Biglow (*CAL*)
Caleb Bingham (*DAB*)
William Hill Brown (*DAB*)
William Cullen Bryant (*DAB*)
Samuel Deane (*DAB*)
Joseph Dennie (*DAB*)
Robert Dinsmoor (*DAB*)
Timothy Dwight (*DAB*)
James Elliot (*DAB*)
David Everett (*DAB*)
Thomas Green Fessenden (*DAB*)
Elijah Fitch (*CAL*)
Hannah Foster (*NAW*)
John S. J. Gardiner (*DAB*)
Fitz-Greene Halleck (*DAB*)
Thaddeus Mason Harris (*DAB*)
David Hitchcock (*CAL*)
Edward Hitchcock (*DAB*)
Enos Hitchcock (*DAB*)
St. John Honeywood (*CAL*)
Lemuel Hopkins (*DAB*)
David Humphreys (*DAB*)

William Jenks (*DAB*)
Samuel Lorenzo Knapp (*DAB*)
Henry C. Knight (*DAB*)
Joseph Brown Ladd (*DAB*)
John Lathrop (*DAB*)
Enoch Lincoln (*DAB*)
Sarah Wentworth Morton (*NAW*)
Judith Sargent Murray (*NAW*)
Selleck Osborn (*DAB*)
Robert Treat Paine (*DAB*)
John Pierpont (*DAB*)
Jonathan Plummer (*DAB*)
Charles Prentiss (*CAL*)
Samuel Randall (*DAB*)
Susanna Rowson (*NAW*)
Jonathan M. Sewall (*DAB*)
Elihu Hubbard Smith (*DAB*)
Solomon Southwick (*DAB*)
Isaac Story (*DAB*)
Joseph Story (*DAB*)
Tabitha Tenney (*NAW*)
Eliza Townsend (*CAL*)
John Trumbull (*DAB*)
William Tudor (*DAB*)
Royall Tyler (*DAB*)
William B. Walter (*CAL*)
Mercy Otis Warren (*NAW*)
Phillis Wheatley (*NAW*)
Elhanan Winchester (*DAB*)
Sarah S. B. K. Wood (*NAW*)
Samuel Woodworth (*DAB*)

* Volume 1 of the much more comprehensive compendium of *American Women Writers*, ed. Lina Mainiero (New York: Ungar, 1979), includes no additional figures that meet the other three criteria.

NOTES

1. Russel Nye, *The Cultural Life of the New Nation* (New York: Harper, 1960), p. 251. For some examples of the viewpoint to which Nye refers, see Barrett Wendell, *A Literary History of America*, 3rd ed. (New York: Scribners, 1900), pp. 117–36; Fred Lewis Pattee, *The First Century of American Literature* (New York: Appleton, 1935), pp. 263, 266; and Robert Spiller, *The Cycle of American Literature* (New York: Macmillan, 1955), pp. 27–29. In the *Literary History of the United States* (New York: Macmillan, 1946), I, 129–30, Spiller speaks of the "false dawn of the nineties and the 'dark ages' which followed"; this idea is repeated in later editions and in *The American Literary Revolution*, ed. Robert Spiller (New York: Doubleday, 1967), p. 4. Indeed it is still common to dismiss early national period literature in sweeping terms; see Emily Stipes Watts, *The Poetry of American Women from 1632 to 1945* (Austin: Univ. of Texas Press, 1977), p. 29: "the literary output of [the last half of the eighteenth century] is a national embarrassment." At the same time, there is a small but growing number of scholars who have taken the period more seriously. In addition to Nye, some of those whose work has helped me most in preparing this paper are William Hedges, Lewis Simpson, Benjamin Spencer, William Charvat, Linda Kerber, Lewis Leary, and Kenneth Silverman. I want particularly to thank Hedges, Robert Richardson, and Peter Shaw for supplying me with copies or abstracts of their papers delivered at the 1979 Modern Language Association symposium on "American Literature, 1785–1815." As short theoretical overviews of the period, I particularly recommend William Hedges, "Toward a Theory of American Literature, 1765–1800," *Early American Literature*, 4 (1969), 5–14; Lewis Simpson, "The Satiric Mode: The Early National Wits," in Louis Rubin, ed., *The Comic Imagination in American Literature* (New Brunswick: Rutgers Univ. Press, 1973), pp. 49–61; and Lewis Simpson, "Literary Ecumenicalism of the American Enlightenment," in A. Owen Aldridge, ed., *The Ibero-American Enlightenment* (Urbana: Univ. of Illinois Press, 1971), pp. 317–32.

2. Lewis Simpson, ed., *The Federalist Literary Mind* (Baton Rouge: Louisiana State Univ. Press, 1962), pp. 3–9. The Emerson quotation, from *Journals and Miscellaneous Notebooks* (Cambridge: Harvard Univ. Press, 1960–), XIII, 115, is quoted approvingly by V. L. Parrington in *Main Currents in American Thought* (New York: Harcourt, 1927), II, 317, following an indictment of turn-of-the-century New England literati as "blind sailors navigating the Dead Sea of Federalist Pessimism" (II, 278).

3. Among the many studies that discuss and compare the impact of Neoclassical and Romantic aesthetics upon American literary culture, the most helpful to me has been Benjamin Spencer, *The Quest for Nationality: An American Literary Campaign* (Syracuse: Syracuse Univ. Press, 1957).

4. This kind of thinking is basic to Perry Miller's seminal "From Edwards to Emerson" (1940; rpt. *Errand into the Wilderness* [Cambridge: Harvard Univ. Press, 1956, pp. 184–203]), and has in general been reinforced by the renaissance in Puritan studies that Miller, Morison, and Murdock inspired. Without intentionally disparaging

American Neoclassicism, works like Sacvan Bercovitch's otherwise excellent *Puritan Origins of the American Self* (New Haven: Yale Univ. Press, 1975) tend to underplay the significance of the Neoclassical phase of New England taste in their attempt to establish linkages between Puritanism and the great American Romantics. A number of such studies skip over the Federalist era altogether. Austin Warren's *The New England Conscience* (Ann Arbor: Univ. of Michigan Press, 1966) is one of many examples.

5. Nina Baym's *Woman's Fiction* (Ithaca: Cornell Univ. Press, 1978) gives an authoritative account of the leading American practitioners of the genre that used to be called the "domestic" or (less accurately) the "sentimental" novel. The career of its stereotypical heroine compares most interestingly to that of Tenney's Dorcasina Sheldon, especially when one bears in mind the overall similarities and differences between Tenney's novel and its British precursors, like New York-born Charlotte Lennox's *Female Quixote*.

6. Leon Howard's pioneering study of *The Connecticut Wits* (Chicago: Univ. of Chicago Press, 1943), pp. 212–30, sets the tone for subsequent criticism of these two poems. For a recent case of selective emphasis on preromantic elements in Neoclassical literature, see Kenneth Silverman's *Cultural History of the American Revolution* (New York: Crowell, 1976), which identifies Wertherism as a key to the 1780s and, I think, overemphasizes the importance of Joseph Brown Ladd, the Rhode Islander turned South Carolinian whom Silverman calls "the first American romantic poet" (p. 491). See William Hedges' comments on this subject in his review in *Early American Literature*, 13 (1978), 137, which also very justly praises the impressive overall achievement of Silverman's work.

7. Perry Miller, "Emersonian Genius and American Democracy," *New England Quarterly*, 26 (1953), 27–44, is a distinguished example of this kind of thinking.

8. This statement is based on examination of Charles Evans' *American Bibliography* for the last quarter of the eighteenth century, as well as the Shaw-Shoemaker *American Bibliography* (1801–1819). For some corroborating composite statistics, see William Charvat, *The Profession of Authorship in America, 1800–1870*, ed. Matthew J. Bruccoli (Columbus: Ohio State Univ. Press, 1968), p. 35.

9. The *DAB* index is notoriously defective. Herman Melville, for instance, is not listed under "Novelist." I assume, however, equal incompetence for all geographical areas.

10. Howard Mumford Jones, *O Strange New World* (New York: Viking, 1967), pp. 227–72, provides a very good summary presentation of the importance of classicism in the early republic. See also Lewis Simpson, "Federalism and the Crisis of Literary Order," *American Literature*, 32 (1960), 253–66, and notes 1–3 above, for other discussions of points made in this paragraph.

11. "Caricature and Satire in Old and New England Before the American Revolution," *Proceedings of the Massachusetts Historical Society*, 88 (1976), 19–34.

12. Robert Arner, "The Connecticut Wits," *American Literature 1764–1789: The*

Revolutionary Years, ed. Everett Emerson (Madison: Univ. of Wisconsin Press, 1977), p. 251.

13. Fisher Ames, "American Literature," rpt. in Spiller, ed., *The American Literary Revolution*, p. 86.

14. Linda Kerber, *Federalists in Dissent: Imagery and Ideology in Jeffersonian America* (Ithaca: Cornell Univ. Press, 1970), pp. 62 ff.

15. "A Plea for Captain John Brown," *Reform Papers*, ed. Wendell Glick (Princeton: Princeton Univ. Press, 1973), p. 129.

16. "The Republican. No. I," *Works*, ed. Seth Ames (Boston: Little, 1854), II, 251–52.

17. For an overview of American Neoclassical satire, in addition to the works already mentioned the following articles by George L. Roth are particularly helpful: "New England Satire on Religion, 1790–1820," *New England Quarterly*, 28 (1955), 246–54; "American Theory of Satire, 1790–1820," *American Literature*, 29 (1958), 399–407; and "Verse Satire on 'Faction,' 1790–1815," *William and Mary Quarterly*, 3rd ser., 17 (1960), 473–85.

18. *Poems by St. John Honeywood* (New York: Swords, 1801), pp. 57, 59.

19. Spencer, p. 39.

20. Quoted (from a 1776 speech of Perez Morton) by James Spear Loring in *The Hundred Boston Orators*, 2nd ed. (Boston: Jewett, 1853), p. 129.

21. Randall Stewart comments insightfully on the "learned" and "restrained" quality of New England writing in "Regional Characteristics in the Literature of New England," *College English*, 3 (1941), 130–35.

22. In addition to the first two articles mentioned in note 1, numerous studies touch upon this doubleness, including the three 1979 M.L.A. papers on literature in the 1790s: William Hedges' "The Age of Shrillness," Peter Shaw's "Revolution, Riot, and Ritual," and Robert Richardson's "The Case Against Prophecy in the 1790s." Stow Persons' "The Cyclical Theory of History in Eighteenth Century America," *American Quarterly*, 6 (1954), 147–63, gives a lucid explanation of the assumptions about history that led the postrevolutionary generation to entertain rival theories of progress and decay. James W. Davidson's *The Logic of Millennial Thought: Eighteenth Century New England* (New Haven: Yale Univ. Press, 1977) gives a learned and persuasive account of the juxtaposition of utopian and holocaust motifs in the period's religious thought.

23. See especially Sacvan Bercovitch's excellent *The American Jeremiad* (Madison: Univ. of Wisconsin Press, 1978), which makes quite explicit his points of dissent from Perry Miller's *The New England Mind: From Colony to Province* (Cambridge: Harvard Univ. Press, 1953), pp. 27–39.

Historic Notes on Life and Letters in Transcendental New England

Joel Myerson

Writing in his journal on November 27, 1837, Ralph Waldo Emerson entered the following questions and answers:

> What is culture? The chief end of man
> What is the apparatus? His related nature
> What is the scale? Himself
> What are my advantages? The total New England.[1]

Emerson had a firm claim on being a good New Englander, one that was much better than that of his fellow Concordian, Henry David Thoreau, who was, after all, merely a second-generation immigrant from the Jersey Isles. He was of the seventh-generation of Emersons in New England, and his forefathers had married into such families as the Bulkeleys, the Moodys, the Blisses, and the Haskinses. Most of his forebears were ministers who took the lead not only in their churches but also in civil and military affairs.

Even though he came of good New England stock, Emerson was still the member of a generation—and probably the last such generation—to stand poised between its English heritage and its uniquely American future, and unsure of the direction in which to go. The "courtly muses of Europe" to which, Emerson complained in 1837, we had "listened too long," still exercised a siren-like fascination for the American populace.[2] Rather than reject this English background, Emerson, in developing his thoughts on New England, began by examining its virtues and defects in order to show that New England—the "America" of the first half of Emerson's life—had taken the best and made it better, while leaving behind the less appealing aspects of English civilization. In so doing, Emerson would slyly imply that many of those things that were original with America and made America great were necessary for the English to aspire toward if they also hoped to secure a high culture. In Emerson's argument, then, the student has overtaken and surpassed the teacher.

Emerson therefore began his consideration of New England with an examination of old England. On a simple level, he saw the New England man as representative of the Old England man in a new location and with new duties, and the American character as the English character exaggerated. On a higher plane, Emerson identified some salient characteristics of the English that had been transported to New England and had been retained with success. These were a strong sense of conscience, a predisposition toward commonsense, an infusion of the religious sentiment into all aspects of life, and a belief in the power of labor as a major stabilizing force of civilization. These characteristics, good to begin with, were made even better as they were adapted to the challenges of New England life. The openness of the country that the first settlers found suggested an infinitude of possibilities; the sparseness of the population required a more introspective way of life; and the democratic government that developed provided the means for a general social as well as personal improvement that would have been impossible in aristocratic England.[3]

This is not to say that New England was merely Old England with corn fields instead of coal mines, or stockades instead of castles, for not only had the New Englanders improved upon what they had brought with them, they left behind the less favorable aspects of English life. The rejection of an aristocracy as the ruling class, the discarding of old traditions and rituals, and other similar breaks with the past all showed the New England desire to establish a country by rules appropriate to that country and its people and not to a land that was far away. Nevertheless, to Emerson there were still parts of the English heritage which he saw as negative that the New Englanders were slow to reject, particularly as regarded the position of the man of letters. As Emerson complained, "the fact seems to me intolerable, what is commonly affirmed, that such is the transcendent honor accorded to wealth and birth, that no man of letters, be his eminence what it may, is received into the best society, except as a lion and a show."[4] There was also the problem of American dependence on

England for its reading and for its critical judgments—America's failure, in other words, to break the literary apronstrings. Too many people were willing to accept English literature as the model to imitate, not to surpass, and to accept English appraisals of literature as gospel rather than as opinion. In tackling this problem in his address on "The American Scholar," Emerson warned that this literary dependence had made the American spirit "timid, imitative, tame," and the American scholar "decent, indolent, complaisant," and he suggested that if "the single man plant himself indomitably on his instincts, and there abide, the huge world will come round to him."[5]

The inability to perceive English defects—and especially the residual ones—disturbed Emerson, for he believed a cardinal virtue of the first New Englanders had been exactly the opposite—the ability to recognize the defects of English life. But what set these people apart from other dissenters was that they acted upon their unhappiness and became not a negative force boring from within but a positive force creating from without. Because, in Emerson's view, these people were, by virtue of their perception, "the most religious & ideal" people in England, it was "natural enough" that in giving expression to their perception by settling in New England, they and their descendants "should be more ideal than Old England."[6]

Those first New Englanders were, of course, the Puritans, and from them Emerson felt his generation had inherited many good qualities. First, there was the "real and overpowering" awe with which the Puritans approached Nature, an awe by which "every new object was magnified," and an awe which would lead Emerson to believe that "Particular natural facts are symbols of particular spiritual facts."[7] Second, there was the lack of aristocracy, which Emerson called "the supreme fortune" of the colonists.[8] Third, there was the way in which Puritanism "chastised" the "ambition in our blood," making man more aware of his responsibilities to his fellow man.[9] And finally, the Puritans knew "that command of Nature comes by obedience to Nature; that reward comes by faithful service; ... that he is greatest who serves best"; or as Emerson would put it, "A man is fed, not that he may be fed, but that he may work."[10]

Emerson has commented upon numerous aspects of Puritan culture as they were carried down to his own generation, especially religion, education, government and reform, and materialism. There

can be no denying that the Puritans were an extremely religious
people, and Emerson once pointed this out by playfully repeating the
words of an old lady who, remembering "these pious people," said of
them "that 'they had to hold on hard to the huckleberry bushes to
hinder themselves from being translated.' "[11] Indeed, it may be argued
whether Emerson's Puritan background was translated into his own
early life or whether his formative years were translated into his
respect for the Puritans. In either case, Emerson's personal background was highly religious: the son and grandson of preachers, he
attended Harvard Divinity School, began his career as a minister, and
counted among his early friends mostly fellow ministers. Not
surprisingly, then, Emerson felt that "religious sentiment" was "the
most refining of all influences," because the "evolution of a highly
destined society must be moral; it must run in the grooves of celestial
wheels."[12] Moreover, the religious sentiment—"always enlarging,
firing man, prompting the pursuit of the vast, the beautiful, the
unattainable"—was "an antidote to the spirit of commerce and of
economy."[13] Religion was also "the Emancipator," for it taught
"equality of all men in view of the spirit which created man."[14] And
religion, to Emerson, was also behind the New Englander's high
estimation of the role of education, since the religious were always
more disposed to give to their children a liberal discipline of books and
schooling.[15]

Emerson continually praised New England "because it is the
country in the world where is the free-est expenditure for education,"
a country where "intellectual entertainment is so within reach of
youthful ambition."[16] The drive for education helped to eliminate
religious prejudices, for each sect wished to educate its members as
well as possible, so as not to be inferior to the others.[17] Government,
too, was affected, and Emerson proudly pointed to "the swelling cry
of voices for the education of the people" as indicating that "Government has other offices than those of banker and executioner."[18]
(There were, however, some problems, as when Sophia Ripley
complained to Emerson that "the young women who came thither [to
Brook Farm] from farms & elsewhere would work faithfully & do
whatever was given them without grumbling, but there was no heart in
it, but their whole interest was in their intellectual culture."[19]) The
system of education in New England was also logical and formed a
pattern of ever-expanding circles: "The town-meeting is, after the

high-school, a higher school."[20] The village lyceum served as another, larger circle in the educational system, and Emerson looked to the lecture room as the true church of the coming time.[21] This "diffusion of knowledge," aided by town meetings, the lyceum movement, and "the cheap press, bringing the university to every poor man's door in the newsboy's basket," was of supreme value in "overrunning all the old barriers of caste."[22] And the spread of education, the making of better citizens for the state, greatly increased political activity and involvement in it.

Emerson's perception of what the government owes to its citizens was simple and direct: "the duty to instruct the ignorant, to supply the poor with work and with good guidance."[23] This sense of governmental responsibility grew out of the Puritans' desire to serve, reinforced by the fact that "our political institutions . . . sprung, within the memory of living men, from the character and condition of the people, which they still express with sufficient fidelity."[24] For Emerson, the character of the people was individualistic and the condition of the people was democratic; such complementary forces shaped New England life and acted as a system of checks and balances. This democracy represented not only a rejection of aristocracy but a rejection as well of all sorts of paternalism by which, as Thoreau put it, a child was kept a child and not made a man. Emerson was worried that this paternalism could come back into government, that "to serve" might be replaced with "to dictate"; such actions as the war with Mexico and the Fugitive Slave Law surely gave Emerson grounds for his concern. And as government attempted to do too much, intruding upon rather than guiding the lives of its citizens, Emerson saw dangers: "The patriarchal form of government readily becomes despotic, as each person may see in his own family. . . . It is very easy to see that this patriarchal or family management gets to be rather troublesome to all but the papa; the sceptre comes to be a crow-bar."[25] Not surprisingly, Emerson looked toward the reform-minded men of the time to counteract any governmental encroachments upon individual freedoms.

Behind Emerson's optimistic belief in reform was his faith in education, for to him the result of education "appears in the power of invention, the freedom of thinking, in the readiness for reforms, eagerness for novelty, even for all the follies of false science."[26] He even saw "the air of mountains and the seashore" as "a potent predisposer to rebellion."[27] That part of the Puritan heritage that continually replaced superfluous old ways with relevant new ones also gave Emerson hope. As he put it: "Boston never wanted a good principle of rebellion in it . . . there is always a minority unconvinced . . . whom the governor and deputies labor with but cannot silence."[28] Truth could not be silenced by mere political expediency.

As Emerson described the intellectual currents of New England in 1842, "Our American literature and history are, we confess, in the optative mood; but whoso knows these seething brains, these admirable radicals, these unsocial worshippers, these talkers who talk the sun and moon away, will believe that this heresy cannot pass away without leaving its mark."[29] This new wave of reformers was partially the result of the decline of some aspects of Puritanism: there "grew a certain tenderness on the people, not before remarked"; children, who "had been repressed and kept in the background," were now "considered, cosseted, and pampered"; and "a reaction of the general mind" occurred "against the too formal science, religion, and social life of the earlier period." These new reformers differed from their ancestors: "Instead of the fiery souls of the Puritans, bent on hanging the Quaker, burning the witch and banishing the Romanist, these were gentle souls, with peaceful and even with genial dispositions, casting sheep's-eyes even on Fourier." But these reformers were also similar to their ancestors in that they were dissatisfied with the status quo and believed that progress did not necessarily mean just going forward. The exteriors may have changed, but the men Emerson called reformers were exactly that—they wished to re-form the basic elements in man's nature to aid in man's moral development, which was not the same as his territorial expansion. As Emerson described them, the "young men were born with knives in their brain, a tendency to introversion, self-dissection, anatomizing of motives."[30]

Emerson very much welcomed these reformers, but only so long as they were true men, "the theorists and extremists, the men who are never contented and never to be contented with the work actually accomplished, but who from conscience are engaged to what the party professes." Man Thinking, Emerson applauded; other forms of man he warned against. Man Borrowing worried him and he declared, "Every project in the history of reform, no matter how violent and surprising, is good when it is the dictate of a man's genius and constitution, but very dull and suspicious when adopted from another." Man Unthinking was even worse: "The criticism and attack on institutions, which we have witnessed, has made one thing plain, that society gains nothing whilst a man, not himself renovated, attempts to renovate things around him: he has become tediously good in some particular but negligent or narrow in the rest; and hypocrisy and vanity are often the disgusting result."[31] The reformation of the individual was clearly for Emerson the starting point of any social reform.

Emerson's individualism naturally made him wary of the New England communitarian reforms and reformers. Whereas the bankers of State Street had warned against the communitarians because they seemed to have "invalidated contracts, and threatened the stability of stocks," Emerson felt that their danger lay in the fact that they had attempted to reform society before reforming themselves, resulting in "a protracted picnic"; or, as he said of Brook Farm, "a French Revolution in small, an age of reason in a patty-pan."[32] Yet even these experiments had a general value for Emerson, not by any concrete accomplishments that were a result of them, but for "the revolution which they indicate as on the way."[33]

To chart a course between false reform and an illusory status quo was the goal of Emerson's own true reform, as well as what he considered the goal of all New England. The false reformers held out no hope; the spirit of their radicalism was "destructive and aimless: it is not loving; it has no ulterior and divine ends, but is destructive only out of hatred and selfishness." On the other hand, Emerson saw "the conservative party, composed of the most moderate, able, and cultivated part of the population," as "timid, and merely defensive of property." It "vindicates no right, it aspires to no real good, it brands no crime, it proposes no generous policy; it does not build, nor write, nor cherish the arts, nor foster religion, nor establish schools, nor encourage science, nor emancipate the slave, nor befriend the poor, or the Indian, or the immigrant." And he concluded: "From neither party, when in power, has the world any benefit to expect in science, art, or humanity, at all commensurate with the resources of the nation."[34] Emerson's antidote to all this may be found in such writings as "New England Reformers," "Politics," and of course "Self-Reliance."

That Emerson would appreciate New England's material prosperity may at first appear odd. After all, it was Emerson who wrote that "Every materialist will be an idealist; but an idealist can never go backward to be a materialist."[35] Emerson is not backsliding or ignoring the hobgoblins of little minds. Although he praises materialism, he also condemns it; moreover, his statements do have an internal consistency: when materialism is used as a means toward the great end of culture, it is good, but when used as both means *and* end, it is bad. Emerson is well aware that we "hear something too much of the results of machinery, commerce, and the useful arts."[36] He even warns that "there is, at present, a great sensualism, a headlong devotion to trade and to the conquest of the continent,—to each man as large a share of the same as he can carve for himself,—an extravagant confidence in our talent and activity, which becomes, whilst successful, a scornful materialism,—but with the fault, of course, that it has no depth, no reserved force whereon to fall back when a reverse comes."[37] But at the same time he takes pride in New England's materialism, taking pride in the increased valuation of the country at every ten years' census, and even expressing what he calls a "sensible relief" when he learns "the destiny of New England is to be the manufacturing country of America."[38]

Behind this apparent ambivalence lies a shrewd and pragmatic, yet idealistic, perception of materialism, a view which holds that the external evidences used to measure success can also be used for the true betterment of mankind. The railroad, which Hawthorne satirized and Thoreau nonchalantly crossed like a cart-path in the woods, became for Emerson "a magician's rod, in its power to evoke the sleeping energies of land and water," for it has "given a new celerity to *time,* or anticipated by fifty years the planting of tracts of land, the choice of water privileges, the working of mines, and other natural advantages."[39] What to some might appear as a machine in the garden, to Emerson becomes a transporter and hastener of other gardens.

Emerson's attitude toward commerce may be taken as another example of his positive view of the uses of materialism. He was aware of its dangers, but he went further by trying to describe its possible benefits. After discussing how Boston's coastal location had made it a point of departure for commerce, Emerson goes on to say that the "most advanced nations are always those who navigate the most," thus neatly equating the spread of trade with the spread of knowledge.[40] Commerce also has the useful effect of enabling the individual to prosper on his own, without the restrictions of a caste system, and in this sense it is anti-feudal.[41]

In general, Emerson felt that New England's materialism was good whenever it was yoked together with its morality, for, as he pointed out in a discussion of Transcendentalist real estate practices, "Moral values become also money values": "A house in Boston was worth as much again as a house just as good in a town of timorous people, because here the neighbors would defend each other against bad governors and against troops; quite naturally house-rents rose in Boston."[42]

Sometimes Emerson's views of New England come together when he is comparing it to other geographical areas. Nowhere is this better demonstrated than in Emerson's comments on the American South. Emerson was not impressed by the Southerners he saw, calling them "haughty, selfish, wilful, & unscrupulous men, who will have their way, & have it. The people of New England with a thousand times more talent, more worth, more ability of every kind, are timid, prudent, calculating men who cannot fight until their blood is up, who have consciences & many other obstacles betwixt them & their wishes."[43] Or, as he puts it in a journal entry, the

> young Southerner comes here a spoiled child with graceful manners, excellent self command, very good to be spoiled more, but good for nothing else, a mere parader. He has conversed so much with rifles, horses, & dogs that he is become himself a rifle, a horse, & a dog and in civil educated company where anything human is going forward he is dumb & unhappy; like an Indian in a church. Treat them with due deference as we often do, and they accept it all as their due without misgiving. Give them an inch & they take a mile. They are mere bladders of conceit. Each snippersnapper of them all undertakes to speak for the entire Southern states. "At the South, the reputation of Cambridge," &c. &c. which being interpreted, is, In my Negro village of Tuscaloosa or Cheraw or St Marks I supposed so & so. "We, at the South," forsooth. . . . Their question respecting any man is . . . How can he fight? In this country, we ask, What can he do?

Emerson's reaction to this is very similar to that of his neighbor Samuel Ripley's in the following dialogue: " 'It must be confessed' said the young man, 'that in Alabama, we are dead to every thing, as respects politics.' 'Very true,' replied Mr. Ripley, 'leaving out the last clause.' "[44]

Yet with all his praise of New England, Emerson saw her defects as well. He complained that "I do not find in our people, with all their education, a fair share of originality of thought."[45] He feared that "America has a bad name for superficialness," and pointed to the popularity of phrenology, with its shallow and swift way of disposing of Nature's sacred secrets, as an example of this.[46] He warned of a love of ritual whereby we "adore the forms of law, instead of making them vehicles of wisdom and justice," and whereby "we have stood a little stupefied by the elevation of our ancestors," instead of declaring "Let us shame the fathers, by superior virtue in the sons."[47] He derogated the "levity and complaisance" of his countrymen, that "they fear to offend, do not wish to be misunderstood; do not wish, of all things, to be in the minority."[48] He saw disadvantages in the "cold and hostile" climate, which "by shutting men up in houses and tight and heated rooms a large part of the year, and then again shutting up the body in flannel and leather, defrauds the human being in some degree of his relations to external nature"; a climate which, by forcing man to provide "fuel and many clothes and tight houses and much food against the long winter, makes him anxiously frugal, and generates in him that spirit of detail which is not grand and enlarging, but goes rather to pinch the features and degrade the character."[49] And he warned that the "cities continually drain the country of the best part of its population: the flower of the youth, of both sexes, goes into the towns, and the country is cultivated by a so much inferior class."[50]

But despite these reservations, Emerson to the end defended his native area, as in this passage from *English Traits* describing a conversation with some Englishmen:

> My friends asked, whether there were any Americans?—any with an American idea,—any theory of the right future of that country? Thus challenged, I bethought myself neither of cau-cuses nor congress, neither of presidents nor of cabinet-ministers, nor of such that would make of America another Europe. I thought only of the simplest and purest minds; I said, "Certainly yes;—but those who hold it are fanatics of a dream which I should hardly care to relate to your English ears, to which it might be only ridiculous,—and yet it is the only true." So I opened the dogma of no-government and non-resistance,

and anticipated the objections and the fun, and procured a kind of hearing for it.[51]

In general, the way in which Emerson viewed New England life is strikingly similar to his usual literary methods. He borrows from his sources whatever he likes, and then rearranges these ideas into a work that goes further—and often in a different direction—than had any of his earlier texts. In writing about New England, Emerson took the best traits of old England and the Puritans, showed why these traits were good ones and also explained why the discarded traits were bad, and forged these traits into an eclectic yet idealized New England character. What results is not so much a portrait of his fellow New Englanders as it is a prescription for a conduct of New England life for himself and others to follow.

NOTES

1. *The Journals and Miscellaneous Notebooks of Ralph Waldo Emerson*, ed. William H. Gilman et al., 14 vols. to date (Cambridge: Harvard Univ. Press, 1960–), V. 442; hereafter cited as *JMN*.

2. "The American Scholar," *Nature, Addresses, and Lectures, The Collected Works of Ralph Waldo Emerson*, ed. Alfred R. Ferguson et al., 2 vols. to date (Cambridge: Harvard Univ. Press, 1971–), I, 114; hereafter cited as *CW*.

3. See "New England" lecture series, lectures I–III, Houghton Library, Harvard University; "Boston," *Natural History of Intellect, The Complete Works of Ralph Waldo Emerson*, ed. Edward Waldo Emerson, 12 vols. (Boston: Houghton, Mifflin, 1903–1904), XII, 205; hereafter cited as *W*. Quotations from the "New England" lecture series are taken from the transcription of the manuscripts kindly provided me by James H. Justus and Wallace E. Williams, editors of the ongoing edition of Emerson's *Lectures* in which the "New England" series will appear, and are used with their permission and that of the Harvard University Library and the Ralph Waldo Emerson Memorial Association.

4. "The Young American," *Nature, Addresses, and Lectures, CW*, I, 243.

5. "The American Scholar," *Nature, Addresses, and Lectures, CW*, I, 69.

6. *JMN*, VIII, 254.

7. "Boston," *Natural History of Intellect, W*, XII, 192; *Nature, Addresses, and Lectures, CW*, I, 17.

8. "Boston," *Natural History of Intellect, W,* XII, 201.

9. "Boston," *Natural History of Intellect, W,* XII, 186.

10. "Boston," *Natural History of Intellect, W,* XII, 205; "Nature," *Nature, Addresses, and Lectures, CW,* I, 12.

11. "Boston," *Natural History of Intellect, W,* XII, 193.

12. "Boston," *Natural History of Intellect, W,* XII, 198; "Civilization," *Society and Solitude, W,* VII, 26.

13. "Boston," *Natural History of Intellect, W,* XII, 197.

14. "Boston," *Natural History of Intellect, W,* XII, 204.

15. "New England" Lecture I.

16. "Education," *Lectures and Biographical Sketches, W,* X, 125; "Domestic Life," *Society and Solitude, W,* VII, 119.

17. "New England" Lecture I.

18. "The Young American," *Nature, Addresses, and Lectures, CW,* I, 235.

19. *JMN,* VIII, 387.

20. "The Fortune of the Republic," *Miscellanies, W,* XI, 527.

21. "New England" Lecture III.

22. "Civilization," *Society and Solitude, W,* VII, 24.

23. "The Young American," *Nature, Addresses, and Lectures, CW,* I, 235.

24. "Politics," *Essays: Second Series, W,* III, 207.

25. "The Young American," *Nature, Addresses, and Lectures, CW,* I, 232–33.

26. "The Fortune of the Republic," *Miscellanies, W,* XI, 527.

27. "Boston," *Natural History of Intellect, W,* XII, 183.

28. "Boston," *Natural History of Intellect, W,* XII, 203.

29. "The Transcendentalist," *Nature, Addresses, and Lectures, CW,* I, 207–208.

30. "Historic Notes of Life and Letters in New England," *Lectures and Biographical Sketches, W,* X, 325, 337, 346, 329.

31. "Boston," *Natural History of Intellect, W,* XII, 202; "New England Reformers," *Essays: Second Series, W,* III, 254, 261.

32. "Historic Notes of Life and Letters in New England," *Lectures and Biographical Sketches, W,* X, 344–45; "Boston," *Natural History of Intellect, W,* XII, 199; "Historic Notes of Life and Letters in New England," *Lectures and*

Biographical Sketches, W, X, 364.

33. "The Young American," *Nature, Addresses, and Lectures, CW*, I, 237.

34. "Politics," *Essays: Second Series, W*, III, 210.

35. "The Transcendentalist," *Nature, Addresses, and Lectures, CW*, I, 202.

36. "The Method of Nature," *Nature, Addresses, and Lectures, CW*, I, 120.

37. "The Fortune of the Republic," *Miscellanies, W*, XI, 531.

38. "New England" Lecture II; *JMN*, V, 301.

39. "The Young American," *Nature, Addresses, and Lectures, CW*, I, 226.

40. "Civilization," *Society and Solitude, W*, VII, 21.

41. "The Young American," *Nature, Addresses, and Lectures, CW*, I, 229.

42. "Boston," *Natural History of Intellect, W*, XII, 206.

43. *JMN*, VII, 473–74.

44. *JMN*, V, 388–89.

45. "Boston," *Natural History of Intellect, W*, XII, 203–204.

46. "Fate," *The Conduct of Life, W*, VI, 5; "New England" Lecture III.

47. "Speech on Affairs in Kansas," *Miscellanies, W*, XI, 258; "Boston," *Natural History of Intellect, W*, XII, 210.

48. "The Man of Letters," *Lectures and Biographical Sketches, W*, X, 255.

49. "Boston," *Natural History of Intellect, W*, XII, 196–97.

50. "The Young American," *Nature, Addresses, and Lectures, CW*, I, 228.

51. "Stonehenge," *English Traits, W*, V, 286–87.

Melville and the Berkshires: Emotion-Laden Terrain, "Reckless Sky-Assaulting Mood," and Encroaching Wordsworthianism

Hershel Parker

Let me offer three propositions as breathlessly as I can; maybe they are not as obvious as they sound. First, the most momentous effect on Herman Melville in the summer of 1850 may have come from the Berkshires, not from Nathaniel Hawthorne. I take the impact of the Berkshires seriously, just as I take the dedication of *Pierre* to Mount Greylock. Second, I think that Melville's great trauma of 1852 occurred in early January, not when the reviews of *Pierre* began appearing in July, and I think that the trauma caused Melville to wreck the unity of *Pierre*; among other things it caused him to write the Enceladus episode, which looks like but is not a companion piece to the earlier use of the Berkshire topography, the Memnon Stone episode. Third, I think Wordsworth was on the edges of Melville's mind from the beginning of the Berkshire experience (after all, his first guest showed up with proofsheets of the first American edition of *The Prelude*); that Wordsworth may have had minor influence on both the Memnon Stone and the Enceladus episodes; and that in the aftermath of *Pierre*, Melville began projecting Wordsworthian attitudes and characters onto the Berkshire landscape.[1]

I think the Berkshires caught Melville off guard when he took his family to Pittsfield for a vacation in July, 1850: he may have forgotten just how dangerous an emotion-laden terrain was to "a very suscepti-

65

ble and peradventure feeble temperament." There in 1831 he had witnessed the reunion of his father and his father's brother Thomas, the ne'er-do-well farmer, who spent time in the Pittsfield jail off and on, for debt, but whom Melville always glamorized as an exile from the court of France: "It was in the larch-shaded porch of the mansion [the house later named Broadhall] looking off, under urn-shaped roadside elms, across meadows to South Mountain. They embraced, and with the unaffectedness and warmth of boys—such boys as Van Dyke painted."[2] After his father died in 1832, Melville spent "the greater portion of a year"[3] (presumably 1834) with his uncle, and in 1837 he boarded uneasily and condescendingly with rustic Yankees while he taught school under Rock, or Washington, Mountain. As a youth he had a favorite vantage point, a rocky elevation from which "he used to linger overlooking the fair plateau on which Pittsfield rears its homes and steeples,"[4] thinking, no doubt, long, long thoughts.

On the 1850 vacation Melville arrived at Pittsfield just as his cousin Robert Melville was about to make an official tour as chairman of the Berkshire Agricultural Society's committee to award Premiums on Crops. On 18 July Melville went off with Bob in his wagon "on a tour of the Southern part of the County of Berkshire, to view the state of the crops." From Lenox they went to Richmond, where from a "high hill" they saw a "fine prospect" of "a crop of rye on a mountain." They put up for the night at a "glorious place" in Lenox, near the Pond, and after waiting out a severe storm the next day, they went to Stockbridge, "& across the Housatonic over 'the plains,' & by Monument Mountain, through Barrington to Egremont," where they spent the night.[5] After looping back to Stockbridge, Melville left his cousin and took the train for Pittsfield, having shared three days of Robert's week-long expedition. He paid for the trip by writing his cousin's report for him, an exuberant spoof. Probably he composed it right away, before he got caught up in socializing and in reading and reviewing Hawthorne's *Mosses from an Old Manse*.

The first paragraph was perfunctory mock-solemn public-occasion prose, interesting mainly for the personal point of view that intrudes toward the end—the sense of how much things had changed in a few years:

> The Committee appointed to award Premiums on Crops have attended to the duty assigned them, and beg leave, before making

a special report of their doings, to premise that, in the prosecution of their duties, they have observed with the highest satisfaction, the manifestations of the spirit of improvements exhibited throughout the county. Frequently has their attention been attracted by the many new and commodious dwellings—by the new and well-filled barns,—by plantations of thriving trees,—and by the numerous, extensive and well cultivated fields of Corn. The contrast between the present appearance of many parts of the County, and that which they exhibited but a few years ago, must strike with admiration, every beholder, who has a mind capable of estimating the value of useful improvement, and show to all, most conclusively, that the efforts of this Society have not been in vain.[6]

Then Melville let himself go in a paragraph celebrating the success of the local warfare against insects and reptiles—mosquitoes and rattle snakes:

Swamps and quagmires, in which the only vegetable productions were alders and ferns, with a few cat-tails interspersed among them as decorations, are now covered with a carpet of herds-grass and clover, and afford exuberant crops of hay. The Committee would be sorry that any words of theirs should give rise to suspicion that they are deficient in the milk of human kindness, and they profess to have as great an aversion to strife as the most enthusiastic members of the Peace Society; yet they cannot withhold their approbation of the determination manifested by the proprietors of these swamps, to exterminate the tribes of insects and reptiles, which, for aught that we know to the contrary, had held a life estate thereof from generation to generation, since the day when Noah, with his numerous family, emerged from the Ark.

Finally, the citified Melville had to praise Nature's wonderful way of using manure:

Another material improvement, which came under the notice of the committee, and to which they allude with pleasure and approbation, is the superior construction of barns, by which not only the comfort of domestic animals is much increased, but greater conveniences for their care, and for the accumulation of manure are attained.

A description of all that the committee noticed during their tour, would extend this report much beyond its proper limits, but they cannot omit this opportunity to impress upon the minds of all their agricultural brethren, the importance of saving every ingredient that can be made to enter into the composition of that substance which renovates exhausted lands, and returns to the earth those particles which have been drawn from it by successive crops; thereby enabling Nature to reinvest herself in her beautiful attire, and to present to her admirers her annual tribute of Flowers and Fruits. The greatest pleasure may be taken by the philosopher and naturalist, (and the farmer *should* be both.) in contemplating that benign process by which ingredients the most offensive to the human senses, are converted into articles that gratify the most delicate taste, and pamper the most luxurious appetite.

This was good family fun, for the hour or two it took to write, and it signalled a mood that kept building for weeks.

In this expansive mood Melville hastened to invite up his city friends, Evert Duyckinck and Cornelius Mathews, wanting to play host in a grand way at his uncle's old place while he still could, it already having been promised in sale to a young New York couple, John and Sarah Morewood. Duyckinck brought along the Appleton proofsheets of *The Prelude* and boasted about editing the *Literary World* at long distance, but his review in the 31 August issue was predictable—a set of random quotations from various parts of the poem intermingled with pious, humbugging commonplaces. He did not read the poem that vacation, and neither did his host. One thing Melville did, rather than seizing those proofsheets greedily, was talk extravagantly about his uncle's farm. Duyckinck reported to his wife that Melville "knows every stone and tree" of the place "& will probably make a book of its features"—a remarkable thing for Melville to have told him, in the middle of writing *Moby-Dick*, and the wording indicates that he really said it—Duyckinck was not an improvisor.[7] With his European trip still fresh in his mind, with *White-Jacket* successfully following the successful *Redburn* (which sold better than its contemptuous author had any right to hope), with the whaling book well under way, and perhaps actually thought of as "mostly done," as Duyckinck reported,[8] Melville experienced the vacation as a triumphant homecoming of the orphan boy who had made good.

Leon Howard thought Melville went on a vacation to look for a place to buy. Maybe he did, but maybe he got the idea after getting there, maybe, to be fair, after meeting Hawthorne. Even after his visit in August, Evert Duyckinck had no notion Melville might settle there, for on 23 September his brother George spoke for both of them in a letter to a friend:

> Herman Melville has taken us by surprize by buying a farm of 160 acres in Berkshire County. It is mostly woodland which he intends to preserve and have a road through, making it more of an ornamental place than a farm. Part of it is on a hill commanding a view of twenty miles, where he intends eventually to build.[9]

Melville's mood was remarkable, for apparently he was also the one—quite uncharacteristically—to tell Sophia Hawthorne that he was "of Scotch descent—of noble lineage—of the Lords of Melville & Leven."[10] That presumably occurred on the "superb moonlight night" when Melville drove up and, according to Sophia, "said he had bought an estate six miles from us, where he is really going to build a real towered house—an actual tower." He was ecstatic, surrendering himself to the intense memories of the past and impressions of the present, all associated with a gorgeous, emotion-laden terrain. (Normally he drove the old Lenox road when he went to see Hawthorne, a route that took him by his old rocky vantage point; small wonder if the collision of times and emotions heightened and perturbed his visits.)

And we have to remember that Melville was young and healthy. He was thirty when he went off on that wagon trip with Robert and turned thirty-one a few days later. At the famous outing on Monument Mountain in August 1850 he boldly seated himself "astride a projecting bow sprit of rock while little Dr Holmes peeped about the cliffs and protested it affected him like ipecac" and while Hawthorne "looked mildly about for the great Carbuncle."[11] The next year on the way to the overnight camp-out on Mount Greylock Melville ascended "the trunk of a tall tree," Mrs. Morewood wrote, with "the agility of a well trained sailor," and from that seat which looked "dangerously insecure" he halloo'd until the Williamstown contingent found its way to his group.[12] This is the man who waded "barefoot through the rushing stream under the North Adams natural bridge," and who thought nothing of going with his sisters and the Morewoods on a casual hike of more than ten miles.[13] In his wagon on mountain excursions he was "a driver daring almost to the point of recklessness," but one who always brought "his ride home to safe conclusion, and his, sometimes terrorized, passengers to a safe landing place."[14] The same witness, J. E. A. Smith, testified in detail to Melville's love of the region; Melville's work routine, he said, was

> often varied by excursions with a friend—or more often with a party of friends, in which the ladies of his own family, those of his friend, Morewood, and their visitors from abroad were sure to be included—to Berkshire localities, interesting either for their beauty, their marked peculiarities or their story, of these he knew many, and was constantly finding more, he was almost extravagantly fond of these excursions. We might say without much exaggeration that they were the great joy of his Berkshire days. Full of jovial life and enthusiasm, he was a most delightful companion, or rather leader, in them; one whose like is rarely found. He invested every scene with new charms, as he dilated upon its beautiful or otherwise interesting features; or rather, it would be more correct to say as he sparkled with spirited and graphic allusions to them. He was not much given to dilation on such occasions; but it was much to be with him when he lightly threw off thoughts suggested by the locality or the incidents of the day, although he seemed as unconscious of any effort as of his breathing or of the beating of his heart. It was as involuntary.[15]

Elsewhere Smith said that "Picnic revelers may be sure that whatever romantic camping-ground they choose in Berkshire, Herman Melville has been there before them, and that its echoes have rung with the laughter and the merry shouts of his rollicking followers."[16] But raucousness was not the dominant mood: after one of his outings to Lake Pontoosuc, Melville told Mrs. Morewood "that each time he came there he found the place possessing new charms for him."[17] When he said in the dedication to *Pierre* that he had received Mount Greylock's "most bounteous and unstinted fertilizations" he was not speaking in what one critic calls "cheerless bravado."[18] On the contrary, he was recording physical and psychological debts we can barely begin to compute. Consider only the topography of *Pierre's* conscious and unconscious mind.

    To local residents the most obvious "fertilization" from the Berkshires was the Memnon Stone or Terror Stone episode, a glamorization of Pittsfield's Balanced Rock. It was a scene guaranteed to give special delight to a few of those residents, the rollicking picnickers. J. E. A. Smith, who took great chauvinistic pride in Melville's use of the Berkshires, later whispered the true story of the naming of the Memnon Stone. A "priestess" (discreetly unnamed, but Sarah Morewood) had crawled far under the rock and set her delicate music box playing there, inspiring Melville (identified only as an author) to vandalize a nearby tree with the word "MEMNON"; worse, the party left behind a broken champagne bottle, or a champagne bottle which was subsequently broken.[19]

The episode begins in leisurely fashion, a paragraph on the shape of the Memnon Stone, a paragraph on how it could have remained undiscovered before Pierre found it, a light-hearted page on Pierre's finding some half-obliterated initials on it which his potty old kinsman deciphered as the signature of Solomon the Wise, then a description of Pierre's crawling beneath the vacancy of the higher end, the "spot first menaced by the Terror Stone should it ever really topple." In the habit already of making childish threats and bargains with the gods, Pierre propounds a series of "if" propositions ("if invisible devils do titter at us when we most nobly strive") and concludes with an invitation: if all that, "then do thou, Mute Massiveness, fall on me." Pierre crawls forth, stands haughtily upon his feet, as if he owed thanks to none, and goes his moody way, feeling he has licence to take whatever ambiguous course he will. In a brief appended chapter, Melville considers some of the "subtler meanings" of the stone, particularly the parallel of Memnon, Hamlet, and Pierre as regal youths doomed in their enthusiastic rashness: "The flower of virtue cropped by a too rare mischance." In his state of human, if not divine, unidentifiableness, Pierre walks on through the woods, shunning mankind: "He could not bring himself to confront any face or house; a plowed field, any sign of tillage, the rotten stump of a long-felled pine, the slightest passing trace of man was uncongenial and repelling to him."

It is a controlled episode, despite the melodrama of Pierre's crawling beneath the stone and promulgating conditions by which he would welcome its falling. Melville works in bits of information about Pierre's earlier years, as he has been doing; he marks a new stage in Pierre's mental ferment; he dramatizes and analyzes Pierre's relation to heroic figures of myth and literature; and he proceeds onward to

Pierre's later state of mind in which "all thoughts now left him but those investing Isabel." Meditation keeps pace with peditation, as if they were wedded forever. (According to William Faulkner, peditation is "the science or process of walking—on foot.") By the end of "Intermediate Between Pierre's Two Interviews," Melville has blended outer and inner landscape: "Still wandering through the forest, his eye pursuing its ever-shifting shadowy vistas," there came "into the mind of Pierre, thoughts and fancies never imbibed within the gates of towns," until finally Pierre's interior "thoughtful river" runs, floating mysteriousness up to him. The conclusion of the last chapter is a remarkable evasion—a sublimation—on Pierre's part. Just as the first incestuous glimmerings appear to him, and just because he dimly discerns an incestuous motivation, he causes Isabel to "wholly soar" (for the moment) "out of the realms of mortalness" and become for him "transfigured in the highest heaven of uncorrupted Love." Far from being an isolated descriptive set piece, the Memnon Stone episode is fully incorporated into Melville's relentless tracking of Pierre's psychological processes.

If we believe any published novel is, by definition, a unified work of art (and fully 95% of critics who publish in the learned journals today believe just that), we can devote some moments to reflecting on the Memnon Stone episode as a splendid prefiguring of the later Mount of the Titans episode. I think treatment of these passages as companion pieces would be a waste, because the second was not part of the original plan but was written after one of the most traumatic experiences in Melville's life, what happened to him when he bundled up his new manuscript shortly after Christmas 1851 and carried it down to offer to the Harpers. It was a short book, estimated at 360 pages, in which he had taken a new literary tack; a Kraken book, he had implied to Hawthorne, a "regular romance," he later told Richard Bentley.[20] We do not know what the manuscript consisted of at that time—maybe, just for a guess, about everything that is in the book we have except anything that has to do with Pierre as a writer. We know what the blunt Harper brothers said: they said, all right, we will publish the thing, but you will take 20 cents on the dollar after costs instead of 50 cents on the dollar. The Harpers had offered terms that would not allow Melville to continue as a writer, unless *Pierre* were miraculously to outsell his earlier books tenfold, and to make things worse some influential magazines were saying in the January issue that *Moby-Dick*, on which he had lavished a year and a half, was "a decided retrogression from former efforts"; Ahab and some of the "tributary characters" were mad, and so was the author.[21] Melville began writing his agonies into the manuscript that had been considered complete or nearly complete—an old pattern with him. He wrote so much so fast that before 21 January 1852 Allan Melville, his lawyer-brother, had already felt obliged to tell the Harpers the book had become much larger.[22] Melville probably finished the expansions at home and sent the manuscript off to Allan in mid-February, for Allan most likely turned it over to the Harpers on 20 February, when the contract was signed.

All this has aesthetic implications. Melville drastically altered the manuscript after it was finished or almost finished, belatedly crediting Pierre with a juvenile literary career and then portraying him in the throes of immaturely attempting to write a great book. There is every indication that Melville did almost no rewriting of the Saddle Meadows section of the manuscript, made no attempt to harmonize his late improvisations with his earlier, tightly controlled narrative. "I write precisely as I please," he said, as he began destroying his book by writing his new troubles into it. The finished book is a botch, and should be recognized as such. We should, for instance, stop talking about the unity of *Pierre* provided by this image or that theme—there is no aesthetic unity in the entire book as published, however much unity there is in the first half or so and however much power there is in certain parts of the city section. We should also stop using the singular in talking about Melville's intention or Melville's purpose in *Pierre*. There was in *Moby-Dick*, for all its own botched qualities, a "pervading thought that impelled the book," as Melville said to Hawthorne.[23] A pervading thought—indeed, a more thoroughly pervading thought—impelled the manuscript of *Pierre* that Melville took to New York, but new thoughts pervaded most of what Melville wrote in January and early February 1852 mixed with older thoughts in whatever he retained of the original concluding sections.

The Enceladus passage is surely part of the January-February expansion. It is not a companion piece to the Terror Stone passage. It is more like a redundant, partially superseding afterthought, for in a book as self-consciously overplotted as the first half of *Pierre*, Melville would hardly have passed up the chance in the Terror Stone passage to mention yet another striking feature of the topography, the

Mount of the Titans, so as to prepare the reader for it.

The Enceladus passage consists of some of the finest writing that Melville ever did: the absorption of imagery from Shakespeare's *The Tempest*; the meditation upon Nature as not her own interpreter but merely the supplier of the cunning alphabet which subjective human beings read as they will according to "peculiar mind and mood"; the strategy of involving the reader (wherein Melville moves from "the tourist" to the complicity-spreading "you"); the power of the contrast of man's earthly household peace versus the ever-encroaching appetite for God, a version of the contrasting values of "The Lee Shore" in *Moby-Dick*; the relation of Enceladus to the heaven-assaulting Ahab in *Moby-Dick*; and the awesome lesson that "whoso storms the sky gives best proof he came from thither!" And the climax of Pierre's dream is great Melvillean excess:

> But no longer petrified in all their ignominious attitudes, the herded Titans now sprung to their feet; flung themselves up the slope; and anew battered at the precipice's unresounding wall. Foremost among them all, he [Pierre] saw a moss-turbaned, armless giant, who despairing of any other mode of wreaking his immitigable hate, turned his vast trunk into a battering-ram, and hurled his own arched-out ribs again and yet again against the invulnerable steep.
>
> "Enceladus! It is Enceladus!"—Pierre cried out in his sleep. That moment the phantom faced him; and Pierre saw Enceladus no more; but on the Titan's armless trunk, his own duplicate face and features magnifiedly gleamed upon him with prophetic discomfiture and woe. With trembling frame he started from his chair, and woke from that ideal horror to all his actual grief.

Wonderful. But it is bigger than the context, for in the previous pages Melville has failed to exalt Pierre's own stature so that the vision is appropriate. It is too big for Pierre's britches. It is not too big for Melville's own britches, and in a thoroughly autobiographical book, or even in a book where the hero is capable of thinking anything that the author is capable of thinking, the passage might have been truly overwhelming. Even as it stands, it is a majestic set piece, but its power is partly drained away by its lack of the most profound relation to the immediately surrounding sections and to the book as a whole. For, as Brian Higgins and I say in "The Flawed Grandeur of Melville's *Pierre*,"[24] in focusing on his hero as author, Melville "loses

sight of Pierre the young man attempting to be Christlike but undone
by human flaws. Now he portrays Pierre the embattled demi-god,
whose degradation is an inevitable part of his Titanic greatness:
'gifted with loftiness' he is 'dragged down to the mud,' even literally.''
As we say there, "Melville is sceptical of a world-rejecting Christian
ethic because it destroys the individual who holds to it, but finally
advocates a world-rejecting Titanism equally destructive of the
individual who holds to it. Through many Books he prepares the
reader to expect a catastrophic ending, a disaster that will be the
inevitable result of Pierre's chronometrical sacrifice for Isabel and of
his being merely human. But when the disastrous end comes, Pierre's
state of mind is a 'reckless sky-assulting mood' that Melville admires
as evidence of demi-godliness."[25]

When I say that the Enceladus section is only partially assimilated into the work as a whole, I am not denying its thematic, verbal,
and imagistic links to other parts. But these links are there not because
Melville felt them unconsciously as, or deliberately designed them
as, mutual strengtheners of this section and the rest of the novel;
rather, they are there because all of the book was written during a very
few months, when the pervading thought which impelled the first half
of the book could not be wholly deflected by his later preoccupations,
and when the particular imagery and verbal patterns in Melville's
mind during those months were bound to emerge in whatever he
wrote, just as there are links between the agricultural report, the essay
on Hawthorne's *Mosses from an Old Manse*, and *Moby-Dick*.

I will conclude with looking at one minor aspect of the imagery in
these two scenes, some possible echoes of Wordsworth which may
foreshadow a new way Melville was to find of thinking about himself
and nature and humanity—a way of thinking manifesting itself in the
subdued moods of the next few years. Father Bertels of the Woodstock
Theological Center recently acquired a copy of Wordsworth's poems
which Melville had owned, and Thomas F. Heffernan has described
Melville's annotations and markings in a fine article in *American
Literature*.[26] Melville took this volume with him on his 1860 voyage
to San Francisco, but we do not know how long he had owned it or
whether it was the first or last copy he ever owned. His first known
reference to Wordsworth predates *Pierre*, and the first plain use of a
Wordsworth poem is the travesty of "Resolution and Independence"
in "Cock-A-Doodle-Doo!"—a story probably written a little less

than a year after *Pierre* was published. There the narrator says:

> "Of fine mornings,
> We fine lusty cocks begin our crows in gladness;
> But when eve does come we don't crow quite so
>   much,
> For then cometh despondency and madness."

And in the 1856–1857 journal Melville makes two knowing references to Wordsworth besides recalling, probably from memory, two other lines from "Resolution and Independence."

Without pushing too far, I will make a couple of comparisons. For what it is worth, on a page of *The Excursion*, Book III, which faces a page on which Melville wrote out two lines of Spenser he was reminded of, occurs this passage about the naming of rocks:

> "The shapes before our eyes
> And their arrangement, doubtless must be deemed
> The sport of Nature, aided by blind Chance
> Rudely to mock the works of toiling Man.
> And hence, this upright Shaft of unhewn stone,
> From Fancy, willing to set off her store
> By sounding Titles, hath acquired the name
> Of Pompey's Pillar; that I gravely style
> My Theban Obelisk; and, there, behold
> A Druid Chromlech!"

In the Woodstock copy, Melville did not mark "Humanity," but it just might have affected the "Terror Stone" aspect of the "Memnon Stone." First I will quote the footnote to line six: "The Rocking-stones, alluded, are supposed to have been used, by our British ancestors, both for judicial and religious purposes. Such stones are not uncommonly found, at this day, both in Great Britain and in Ireland." The poem begins this way (in the copy Melville owned):

> What though the Accused, upon his own appeal
> To righteous Gods when Man has ceased to feel,
> Or at a doubting Judge's stern command,
> Before the STONE OF POWER no longer stand—
> To take his sentence from the balanced Block,
> As, at his touch, it rocks, or seems to rock;
> Though, in the depths of sunless groves, no more
> The Druid-priest the hallowed Oak adore;

> Yet, for the Initiate, rocks and whispering trees
> Do still perform mysterious offices!
> And still in beast and bird a function dwells,
> That, while we look and listen, sometimes tells
> Upon the heart, in more authentic guise
> Than Oracles, or winged Auguries,
> Spake to the Science of the ancient wise.

Maybe.

Heffernan pointed out that some lines Melville marked in *The Excursion*, Fifth Book (about the fertilizing moisture which gathers around stones) resemble some lines in the Enceladus passage: "for the rocks, so barren in themselves, distilled a subtile moisture, which fed with greenness all things that grew about their igneous marge." (In "The Piazza" Melville credits "Oberon" with that same bit of lore.) If Melville was thinking about Wordsworth then, he may have remembered these lines from "Resolution and Independence":

> As a huge stone is sometimes seen to lie
> Couched on the bald top of an eminence;
> Wonder to all who do the same espy,
> By what means it could thither come, and whence;
> So that it seems a thing endued with sense:
> Like a sea-beast crawled forth, that on a shelf
> Of rock and sand reposeth, there to sun itself . . . .

Compare, just above the "igneous marge" passage, Melville's description of the long acclivity "thickly strewn with enormous rocky masses, grotesque in shape, and with wonderful features on them, which seemed to express that slumbering intelligence visible in some recumbent beasts—beasts whose intelligence seems struck dumb in them by some sorrowful and inexplicable spell."

In the years just after *Pierre*, Melville often described landscapes which derive a haunting part of their power from human associations with them, a familiar Wordsworthian situation, as in this passage from *The Excursion*, Book I, the last nine lines of which are on a page where Melville checked a line:

> "Beside yon Spring I stood,
> And eyed its waters till we seemed to feel
> One sadness, they and I. For them a bond
> Of brotherhood is broken; time has been

When, every day, the touch of human hand
Dislodged the natural sleep that binds them up
In mortal stillness; and they ministered
To human comfort. Stooping down to drink,
Upon the slimy foot-stone I espied
The useless fragment of a wooden bowl,
Green with the moss of years, and subject only
To the soft handling of the Elements . . . ."

Again and again in "The Encantadas" Melville writes of relics of "vanishing humanity" in the islands, such as (in Sketch 10) "small rude basins in the rocks" which "reveal plain tokens of artificial instruments employed in hollowing them out," the basins serving to catch drops of dew exuding from the upper crevices. In Sketch 8, Norfolk Isle because of Hunilla's sufferings becomes a "spot made sacred by the strongest trials of humanity." The first chapter of *Israel Potter* makes more boldly picturesque use of a Titanic region of decay and desertion on which "the tokens of ancient industry" are seen on all sides. Of course in his own wanderings in the Berkshires Melville found deserted homesites and other evidence of older human occupancy, but Wordsworth's influence may have blended in.

More significant is the sudden appearance of humble, resolute, suffering Wordsworthian cottagers in Melville's writings, from the Merrymusk family in "Cock-A-Doodle-Doo!" to the Coulters in "Poor Man's Pudding" (who, being self-reliant Americans, find themselves worse off than Wordsworth's poor, who can, at the worst, always beg) to Marianna in "The Piazza," the realistic girl whom the narrator finds after such Hawthornesque, Disneyesque mountain climbing. At the end of "The Piazza" the speaker accepts the illusion of the day and does not brood on human misery—until truth comes in with darkness and he is haunted by Marianna's face, "and many as real a story"—stories like "Bartleby," "Benito Cereno," and "The Encantadas," and other stories of 1853–1856, including that of the Revolutionary beggar Israel Potter. Wordsworth helped humanize the Berkshires for Melville, helped teach him "To look on nature, not as in the hour / Of thoughtless youth; but hearing oftentimes / The still, sad music of humanity . . . ." The blows of the early and mid 1850s were brutal—the vicious reception of *Pierre*, failure at office-seeking, humiliating illnesses, shameful indebtedness—so that by the time he wrote *The Confidence-Man* in 1855 and 1856 one strong impulse of Melville's was to mock any fatuously sentimental view of a beneficent Nature. But this mood was not chronic: he interrupted his work on *The Confidence-Man* to write "The Piazza," where a morbid view of Nature is rejected as the "ingrate peevishness" of weary convalescence. Melville said of Pierre that Nature had planted him in the country because she "intended a rare and original development" in him: "Never mind if she proved ambiguous to him in the end; nevertheless, in the beginning she did bravely."[27] The Berkshires did bravely for Melville, confronting him as they did with poignant memories, a setting where he would inevitably begin to dip his angle into the well of his own childhood, after that early ecstatic period when he felt he was drawing some of the best parts of his diverse life together in one charmed circle of ambiguous terrain.

NOTES

1. Quotations from *Pierre* are from the Northwestern-Newberry edition, but they are not footnoted when they come from the two short episodes under discussion, the Memnon Stone episode in Book 7 and the Enceladus episode in Book 25.

2. *The Melville Log*, ed. Jay Leyda (New York: Gordian Press, 1969), I, 48. The quotation in footnote 10 is not in the 1951 edition of the *Log*, but the others are.

3. *Log*, I, 63.

4. *Log*, I, 421.

5. *Log*, I, 379. These are Melville's notes in the front fly-leaves of *A History of the County of Berkshire*, which he had just bought on 16 July 1850.

6. The Northwestern-Newberry edition of *The Piazza Tales and Other Prose Pieces, 1839–1860* (in press), p. 449. The next two quotations are from pp. 449–50 and pp. 450–51. The report was first published in the Pittsfield *Culturalist and Gazette* for 9 October 1850.

7. *Log*, I, 383.

8. *Log*, I, 385.

9. *Log*, I, 396.

10. *Log*, II, 925.

11. *Log*, I, 384.

12. *Log*, I, 424.

13. The wading is in J. E. A. Smith's *Herman Melville*, as reprinted in Merton M. Sealts, Jr.'s *The Early Lives of Melville* (Madison: Univ. of Wisconsin Press, 1974), p. 124; the walking is in *Log*, I, 431.

14. *Early Lives*, p. 136.

15. *Early Lives*, p. 131.

16. *Early Lives*, p. 200 (from Smith's *The Poet Among the Hills: Oliver Wendell Holmes in Berkshire*).

17. Eleanor Melville Metcalf, *Herman Melville: Cycle and Epicycle* (Cambridge: Harvard Univ. Press, 1953), p. 125.

18. Luther Stearns Mansfield, "Melville and Hawthorne in the Berkshires," in *Melville and Hawthorne in the Berkshires: A Symposium*, ed. Howard P. Vincent (Kent: Kent State Univ. Press, 1968), p. 21.

19. *Early Lives*, pp. 147, 195, 197.

20. *The Letters of Herman Melville*, eds. Merrell R. Davis and William H. Gilman (New Haven: Yale Univ. Press, 1960), p. 142, Melville's 17? November 1851 letter in response to Hawthorne's praise of *Moby-Dick*, and *Letters*, p. 150.

21. The reviews are conveniently available in *"Moby-Dick" as Doubloon* (New York: W. W. Norton, 1970); the quotations here are from pp. 80 and 83. For a comparison of the language in reviews of *Moby-Dick* with the language used by *Pierre*'s reviewers, see my "Why *Pierre* Went Wrong," *Studies in the Novel*, 8 (Spring, 1976), 14–16.

22. See "Why *Pierre* Went Wrong," p. 11, as well as my "Contract: Herman Melville's *Pierre*," *Proof*, 5 (1977), 27–44, which contains reproductions of the contract, of draft passages, and of Allan Melville's 21 January 1852 letter to the Harpers.

23. *Letters*, p. 143.

24. In *New Perspectives on Melville*, Faith Pullin, ed. (Edinburgh: Univ. of Edinburgh Press, 1978), p. 189.

25. "Flawed Grandeur," p. 192.

26. "Melville and Wordsworth," *American Literature*, 49 (1977), 338–51. The edition Melville had was *The Complete Poetical Works of William Wordsworth*, ed. Henry Reed (Philadelphia: James Kay, Jun. and Brother, 1839). My quotations are from Melville's copy, which I examined through the courtesy of Father Bertels.

27. *Pierre*, p. 13.

Earlier Black New England:
The Literature of the
Black I Am

William H. Robinson

Appropriating Thomas DeQuincey's distinction between the literature of knowledge and the literature of power to the rationale for
their use of various pre-eighteenth-century American writings, Davis,
Frederick, and Mott point out that American literature most certainly
did not begin with fully matured, aesthetically developed eighteenth-
century novelists, short story writers, poets, and dramatists; that,
rather, the literature grew from the sprawling mass of earlier written
expressions—promotional tracts, histories, letters, diaries and journals, sermons, philosophical and political science statements—all
specimen of the literature of knowledge, whose chief function,
DeQuincey wrote, was to inform, to teach. To appreciate more fully
the literature of power of the eighteenth century and thereafter, these
editors remind their readers that a more serious regard of such earlier
writings is in order. After a display of the work of more than 100
writers, in some 2000 pages, the editors end their book with but a
single excerpt from a single black American writer: 5½ pages from
Richard Wright's *Black Boy* (1945).[1] This need to give value to pre-
eighteenth-century American writings was repeated in Cady, Hoffman,
and Pearce in 1956. Here the literature of knowledge is described as

> the swaying of the reader to a new and more correct opinion, . . .
> in short, a literature of survival . . . one which rose from the
> necessity to make old ways of acting and believing serve in a new
> situation; from the necessity to make a home at once for body

and spirit, in a new, frightening yet promised land. . . .[2]

Although this description almost perfectly fits early black New England writing, this anthology, after some 1700 pages, and 100 writers, concludes with one excerpt from one black American author: 5 pages from Ralph Ellison's *Invisible Man* (1952). As is commonly known, there were other anthologies and textbooks that did not include the work or mention of any black writers. This omission of black writing from literary anthologies might easily lead some curious readers to deduce that black Americans had produced no literature worthy of reproduction. This is most assuredly not the case.

To be sure, black American literature, especially early black American literature, is not a phenomenon of huge proportions; blacks in and out of New England have not been inclined to the written word as much as they have favored the spoken word. However, blacks did write and in all of the various genres of prose and poetry. Here there is space enough only to glimpse the writings of early black New England, that written by those native to, or living in, or published in New England before the 1920s developed, when began the Harlem Renaissance, for many the true beginning of black American literature.

On the aesthetic level of the literature of power, distinguished by its conscious and formal intentions to move the reader through crafted manipulation of the affections of pleasure and sympathy, literary historian Robert Bone has counted some twenty-four novels and novelettes written by blacks between 1853 and 1921, only a half dozen of which were published in New England.[3] Bone has also located a dozen collections of black-written short stories published between 1895 and 1920, only three of which were brought out on New England presses.[4]

Black-written drama goes back at least to 1858 when Boston's William Wells Brown published *The Escape*,[5] although he had written and several times publicly read an earlier melodrama, *Experience* (1856), but this is non-extant.[6] There were other, non-extant plays as early as 1823, for instance, when Henry Brown of the New York African Theater staged his *Drama of King Shotaway*, "founded on facts, taken from the Insurrection of the Caravs on the island of St. Vincent. Written from experience by Mr. Brown."[7] From these times until Boston's Angelina Weld Grimke's play, *Rachel*, won a prize for craftsmanship and was published in 1920, the development of early black drama, including that in New England, was a sorry spectacle. Struggling in New York City, sustained legitimate theatre was beyond the means of enough New England blacks; also it must be remembered that it was not until after the Civil War that even Boston blacks were permitted, more or less, to enter all of that city's playhouses. Would-be serious black drama was discouraged, and "coon" shows and minstrelsy and crude musicals were popularized, even imitated, by whites, attracting talented black writers otherwise without viable outlets. One black New Englander did manage to make the most of this kind of situation. Exploiting the white New England craze for minstrelsy and black vaudeville, extremely popular Billy Ashcroft, of Providence, Rhode Island, where Ashcroft Street is named for him, earned enough money as one half of a team billed as "the Champion Clog Dancers of the World" to soon leave America. He travelled to England where he married a local girl and later bought his own theater in Belfast, Ireland, and became financially well-to-do.[8]

During the nineteenth century, roughly from the time of Phillis Wheatley (died 1784) and Paul Laurence Dunbar (died 1906), "at least 130 black men and women published poetry in America," or so reports one source.[9] However, fewer than two dozen volumes of this verse were published by black New Englanders. Many of these poets contributed only a few poems, less than would make up a decent anthology or collection. On the other hand, if one were to count as separate the variations of nineteen of the thirty-eight poems in her *Poems on Various Subjects, Religious and Moral* (London, 1773), and include other manuscript poems only recently published, and add her broadsides, pamphlets, and pieces published in colonial newspapers and magazines, Phillis Wheatley (Peters) alone might be said to have composed over one hundred poems and to have published about fifty pieces in her lifetime.

On the level of literature as information or knowledge, the slim output of New England blacks of the pre-Harlem Renaissance period swells a bit, for then consideration can be given to such writings as petitions, letters, essays, addresses, diaries and journals, histories, slave narratives, and even the extant proceedings of early black self-help organizations. Precious few seventeenth- and eighteenth-century black-written or black-dictated petitions, usually for personal or group freedom, were published in their own times. It would remain for

Aptheker in 1951 to unearth and publish over 200 little known or unknown documents of black American life dating from 1661 to 1910, including a dozen eighteenth-century petitions and even more nineteenth- and early twentieth-century pieces written by black New Englanders.[10]

Corresponding secretary for the Underground Railroad, William Still in 1872 published his *Underground Railroad*, made up largely of brief narratives of the tales of over 800 escaped slaves, whom he helped to freedom. More than a dozen of the many letters here were dictated or written by fugitive slaves newly relocated (and often newly renamed) in various parts of New England. These poignant letters thank Still for his services, describe their lives as free persons, and ask for more help in securing the freedom of family members left behind and still in slavery. Upon reaching New Bedford, Massachusetts, safely, barely literate Robert M'coy, alias William Donar, would write:

> Dear Sir — I embrace this opertunity to inform you that I received your letter with pleasure. . . . I rejoise to hear from you i feel very much indetted to you for not writing before but i have been so bissy that is the cause i rejoise to heare of the arrival of my wife, and hope she is not sick from the rolin of the sea and if she is not, pleas to send her on here Monday with . . . a rifall [i.e., rifle] to gard her up to my residence . . . i would come but i am afraid yet to venture. . . .[11]

Another fugitive was elected to the New Bedford City Council and later ran for a congressional seat as a Virginian.[12] Dean of black American scholars, Carter G. Woodson collected 234 letters which he published in 1926. More than 60 of these letters were written by blacks of New England.[13] Philip Foner spent twenty-five years collecting and editing over 500 of Frederick Douglass's letters. In various repositories, modern scholars are finding even more such letters concerning other early black New Englanders. Since 1974, for instance, almost a dozen manuscript letters written by Phillis Wheatley have been discovered and published by various hands. In 1972 Sheldon Harris published a generous sampling of letters written by and to Paul Cuffe, wealthy black sea captain of Westport, Massachusetts.[14]

Diaries or journals out of early black New England are very few. In 1973 Dorothy Sterling published most of the slim "diary" of

Newport, Rhode Island's Caesar Lyndon (died 1794), which runs only from 1765 through 1770.[15] Containing only twenty-one entries, and running for less than a month—from July 26, 1785, until August 15, following—when he broke off writing for reasons unknown even to his biographer, Reverend Lemuel Haynes's journal is of even more limited value.[16] Logging his activities as he captained his favorite ship, *Traveller*, from Westport, Massachusetts, to Sierra Leone, to London and back to Sierra Leone, and finally back to Westport during the year 1811–1812, Paul Cuffe's journal has been published almost completely.[17] In 1953 Ray Billington edited, from manuscript and typescript, *The Journal of Charlotte Forten*, covering the musings and reflections on social intercourse between a genteel, highly educated "woman of color" school teacher in Salem and prominent New Englanders from 1854 through 1864. Billington notes but does not publish another journal kept by Miss Forten, intermittently covering the years 1885–1892 and housed at Howard University.[18]

Having lain in manuscript for almost two hundred years in various Newport, Rhode Island, black homes and churches, and, after 1963, in the vaults of the Newport Historical Society, the proceedings and correspondence of the Free African Union Society and the African Benevolent Society have been used sparingly by only a few recent scholars. In 1976 both sets of papers were edited and published under the auspices of the Urban League of Rhode Island. Although there are many random pages missing from both sets of manuscript proceedings, creating gaps in the chronology, and although the spelling and grammar are in editorial need, these proceedings uniquely span the years of black Rhode Island life from 1780 through 1824. They afford uncommonly rare original views, strategies, desperations of early black New Englanders who tried, in their unschooled ways, to cope with the galling difficulties of building a segregated church community among those who weekly preached Christian brotherhood; with frightened and despairing back-to-Africa aspirations of some who, intimidated, agreed with those whites who proclaimed that blacks and whites simply could never peacefully co-exist; with trying to supply relevant education for their young; with trying to grasp some semblance of human, meaningful lives for themselves and their posterity in a country that often sought to ignore or deny them.[19]

In his study *Many Thousand Gone*, Charles Nichols lists thirty slave narratives and autobiographies, written between 1760 and 1919. There are more narratives elsewhere. Whether simply dictated by an illiterate fugitive, or written down by a semi-literate black and later edited by a friendly amanuensis, or written completely by a literate ex-slave, slave narratives constitute an original American literary genre. In adapted forms, many of them were often written down sometime after they had been otherwise delivered, orally, from platforms and pulpits along the New England abolitionist lecture circuit. Designed to engender revulsion against chattel slavery, these first-hand accounts of the physical and emotional brutalities—whippings, tortures, disfigurements, forced separation by auction from parents and family—sold for 25¢ in paper and $1.50 hardbound. They flourished from the 1830s through the 1850s and intermittently thereafter into the early twentieth century. Some of them were so vividly and powerfully written that they were translated into several foreign languages, including Dutch, German, French, and Celtic, or they reached multiple American editions. Said to have been the human model for "Uncle Tom," Josiah Henson brought out his *Truth Stranger Than Fiction*, with an introduction by Mrs. Harriet Beecher Stowe, which is said to have sold 100,000 copies. The first of three Frederick Douglass autobiographies went into nine editions in London during its first year of publication.[20]

Not all of these narratives were written for the same propagandistic anti-slavery purpose. James Mars, of Canaan, Connecticut, said he wrote his *Life* to oblige his free-born sister and his free-born children. They were all curious to know something about American slavery, especially slavery in Connecticut, which Mars is notably anxious to make known was his lot.[21] Having been owned by ten mean masters, William Grimes fled to Connecticut, where "after six years, he was recognized by some of his former master's friends, taken up, and compelled to purchase his freedom with the sacrifice of all that he had," which included his own home in Litchfield. Ostensibly he published his *Life* at his own expense, hoping thereby to recoup some of his financial losses.[22] Forced to purchase his freedom repeatedly from three different masters—one of them flatly refused to honor his promise—and the freedom of his wife, his son, and grandchild, Moses Grandy wrote his *Narrative* to help him "raise $100 to buy the freedom of my sister Mary, who is a slave at Elizabeth City, N.C. Her master says he will take that sum for her."[23] From Salem, Massachusetts, Jacob Stroyer published his *Sketches* in 1879 in hopes of securing tuition money enough to allow him to complete theological studies at Talladega College, Alabama.[24] Almost seventy years old and blind, William J. Brown brought out his *Life* because he needed the money.[25] Nancy Prince, from Newburyport, Massachusetts, fell onto hard times after having lived for nine years with her husband, a servant for the Russian Tsar Alexander from 1824 to 1833. A widow, she was obliged to leave Russia and her own servants and return to America, where she was a missionary to Jamaica, but was almost helpless as she lost the use of her arms. Therefore, she writes in the preface to "the third edition of my narrative, . . . I take this method that by the sale I hope to obtain the means to help supply my necessities. . . ."[26]

Speeches and formal addresses were plentiful for interested early black New England audiences, who packed churches and public halls to see and hear their orators declaim on the evils of slavery, the slave trade, segregated public transportation, segregated churches and schools, the Fugitive Slave Law of 1850, the pros and cons of colonization, threats to disenfranchise blacks in various states, and other issues of importance to them. A number of these pieces were published early on, perhaps the earliest being by an ex-slave, Caesar Sarter, living in Newburyport, Massachusetts. Sarter's remarks occupy more than half of the front page of the August 17, 1774, issue of *The Essex Journal and Merimack Packet: or The Massachusetts and New Hampshire General Advertiser*, forthrightly condemning the hypocrisy of freedom-loving Christian slaveholders. Rehearsing all of the obvious reasons for black freedom, Sarter concludes his complaint with a plea for the "honorable assembly" to free all blacks, grant them deeds, and relocate them "in some back part of the country."

Carter Woodson collected and edited seventy specimen orations in a work that includes more than a dozen selections written by or delivered to black New Englanders.[27] In *The Life and Writings of Frederick Douglass*, Foner has gathered sixty-five of this speaker's remarks, several of which first appeared in Boston's *Liberator*.[28] In *The Voice of Black America: Major Speeches by Negroes in the United States 1797–1971*, Foner assembled one hundred and twenty-five selections, and more than two dozen of them were composed and rendered by or for pre-renaissance New Englanders.[29] There are still other addresses uncollected by either Woodson or Foner. Several of the more important ones might include *Charge*

Delivered to the Brethren of the African Lodge, on the Twenty-Fifth of June, 1792, in Charlestown, by Boston's Prince Hall, founder of black American Masonry;[30] William Wells Brown's *Lecture Delivered Before the Female Antislavery Society of Salem. At Lyceum Hall, Nov. 14, 1847*; [31] Booker T. Washington's speech at Harvard University;[32] and an early sermon preached by a newly ordained black Methodist minister to the first African Masonic lodge in America.[33] The first American-born woman to speak in public and leave behind extant texts of her offerings, Hartford-born Frances Maria W. Stewart, published two collections: *Productions of Mrs. Maria W. Stewart*,[34] and *Meditations from the Pen of Mrs. Maria W. Stewart, Negro*.[35] Stridently pious to annoyance, forever scolding her audiences for their racial shortcomings and "immoral excesses," Mrs. Stewart was so self-righteously driven that she alienated herself from any kind of a following.

Curiously, or perhaps not curiously at all, throughout all of this literature, a few slave narratives excepted, there is not much attention devoted to particularizing black New England life until 1900 and thereafter. This omission may strike some as unusual, even curious, when it is remembered that, in dramatic contrast to harsh Southern plantation slavery, New England servitude was benign; that by 1784 all of the area's states had legally provided for the abolition of domestic slavery; that New England was a favorite target locale for runaway slaves; that New England was the home of uncounted radical abolitionists, some of whom publicly vowed to suffer ostracization, bodily injury, even death, if necessary, to purge human chattel slavery from the land, and that education for blacks was generally encouraged. New England colleges were the first in the country to enroll and graduate blacks. Despite these and other laudable features of New England, area black life was not extensively detailed until Maine-born, Boston-educated and reared Pauline Hopkins published her first novel, *Contending Forces*, a melodramatic story of the newly emerging black middle class of late nineteenth-century Boston.[36]

One reason it took so long for area blacks to write of their daily lives and loves may easily have been that it took so long for the costly creation of a worthwhile life to write about. Early on it was a grim truism that many free blacks were often far worse off economically than slaves or servants whose masters would at least provide for them in times of need. Early on, New England blacks knew that some of these avid and dedicated abolitionists who uncompromisingly refused to live in a land that sanctioned black (or red or yellow) slavery also uncompromisingly refused to live in a land in which blacks (or reds or yellows) were to be routinely regarded as intellectual, economic, political, and social equals. Early on, free New England blacks were among the very first to feel the impact of De Tocqueville's dictum, "in the United States people abolish slavery for the sake not of the Negroes but of the white man."[37] Early on, such New England racism so disillusioned some blacks that they were driven to conclude that prospects for blacks in white America would indeed never be bright and that the universally wretched conditions of blacks were, as some whites had preached, divinely ordained, heavenly wrath inflicted upon a sinful heathen people. Shattered, handfuls of mortified blacks were prompted to consider emigration to Africa, to Central America, to Haiti, anywhere that, they fancied, might afford them a more compatible milieu, anywhere that they could entertain hopes of living out meaningful, redemptive Christian lives. Thus members of the Free African Union Society of Newport, Rhode Island, could record in their proceedings of 1789:

> We, taking into consideration the calamitous state into which we are brought by the righteous hand of GOD, being strangers & outcasts in a strange land, attended with many disadvantages and evils, with respect to living, which are like to continue on us and on our children while we and they live in this country, and the yet more wretched state of many hundreds of thousands of our brethren, who are in the most abject slavery, in the West Indies, and in the American States . . . and are sunk down in ignorance, stupidity and vice, and considering the unhappy state and circumstances of our brethren, the nations in Africa, from whom we sprang, being in heathenish darkness & barbarity, and are, and have been for many years, many of them, so foolish and wicked as to sell one another into Slavery, by which means many Millions have either lost their lives, or been transported to a Land of Slavery; and whereas GOD has been pleased of late to raise up many to compassionate and befriend the African, not only in promoting their freedom . . . but by proposing . . . to effect their return to their own country and their settlement there, where they may be more happy than they can be here . . . We . . . think there is a special and loud call to us, and all Blacks in

America to seek God . . . humbly to confess the sins of our
fathers, and our own sins; and to acknowledge the righteousness
of GOD in bringing all these evils on us and our children &
brethren & earnestly to cry to GOD for the pardon of our
sins. . . .[38]

Under the leadership of seventy-five-year-old ex-slave Newport
Gardner, twenty-six fellow frustrated black Rhode Islanders jour-
neyed to Boston, from where they and a tiny band of other area blacks
set sail aboard the brig *Vine* on January 26, 1826, arriving in Liberia
the next month. Within two years, however, Gardner and his
followers all succumbed to "African fevers."

Even before the unfortunate, sad adventure of these hapless Rhode
Islanders, there had been others interested in emigration to other parts
of West Africa. Paul Cuffe (1795–1817) was born on Cuttyhunk,
reared in Westport, Massachusetts, where, a free-born black, he rose
from poverty to wealth by virtue of hard work, a shrewd business
sense, and his skills as a shipbuilder. He became the owner of his own
fleet of six whaling and merchant ships. He spent much of his life and
effort in philanthropy for his white, Quaker neighbors—on his own
land he erected the first school building in Westport in 1797; a Quaker
Meeting house erected in 1813 was paid for mostly by Cuffe, and still
stands—but, a black man, he was refused the right to vote. A petition
to the general assembly in 1780, and one to the local authorities in
1781, were both denied. Gradually, Cuffe began to think of living a
more complete life, if not in bigoted America then elsewhere. In 1811,
aboard his flagship, *Traveller*, he sailed to Sierra Leone to explore
long-considered missionary and commercial and colonizing possibilities. On a second trip there, in 1815, he transported thirty-eight
disaffected black Americans almost entirely at his own expense of
over $2,000. When he died he left behind a modest body of writing
made up of scrapbooks, letter-press notebooks, a journal logging his
trip to Sierra Leone-to London-to Sierra Leone-to Westport in
1811–1812, a "Brief Account/ Of The/ Settlement and Present
Situation/ of/ The Colony/ of/ Sierra Leone . . ." (1812), and a body
of letters written by and to Cuffe dating from 1780 through 1817. All
of these papers may be found in the New Bedford Free Public Library.

All of the money wastefully spent by the American Colonization
Society to remove merely a few hundreds of blacks annually to Africa
could more judiciously be spent on planting "twice as many *thou-*

sands in Central America, with everything requisite for their rapid progress. . . ." So wrote James M. Whitefield as editor of the pro-colonization *African-American Repository* in 1858. Born in Exeter, New Hampshire, in 1822, Whitefield, although free, early became disgusted with poverty-stricken, racially circumscribed black New England life and moved to Buffalo, New York, where he earned something of a living as a barber. He earned more of a reputation as a poet, notably with his single volume *America and Other Poems* (1835). He was also known as a militant separatist who loudly advocated voluntary emigration of American blacks to Central America. He lectured on this matter, and publicly argued against integrationist-minded Frederick Douglass, in letters that were published in 1853. He moved to the West Coast, where, still barbering, he continued also to publish poems, several in the *San Francisco Elevator* from 1867 through 1870. He died in April of the following year. Recent research has shown that the American West was apparently congenial to Whitefield's robust temperament. He became involved in black and white civic life, accepting election to a jurorship in Elkho County, Nevada, and participating in various literary and social activities of the Elkho Republican Club, and said less and less about emigration. In fact, his last known poems are described as downright patriotic.[39]

A one-time resident of Burlington, Vermont, and New Haven, Connecticut, James T. Holly (1829–1911) was still another early black New Englander who chafed at restrictive white domination. Continuously he agitated for emigration, at first to Liberia, then to Canada, and, finally, to Haiti, where he settled after 1855 and died. Holly left a number of forcefully written, if not always closely reasoned, letters and addresses, some of which were published in their time with others in the columns of *The Voice of the Fugitive* (1851), a Toronto newspaper, now in the Manuscript Division of the Library of Congress, and elsewhere. A dedicated anti-papist, committed to substituting Protestantism for Catholicism in Haiti, Holly saw emigration to that island republic as a matter of timely destiny for black American Christian warrior colonists:

> Civilization and Christianity are passing from the East to the West; and in their pristine splendor will only be rekindled in the ancient nations after they have belted the globe in its westward course and revisited the Orient again. . . . God, therefore, in

permitting the accursed slave traffic to transplant so many
millions of the race to the New World and educing therefrom
such a Negro nationality as Haiti indicates that we have work to
do here in the Western world, which in his own good time shall
shed its Orient beams upon the fatherland of the race....[40]

For complex reasons, the overwhelming majority of black Americans,
including most of those throughout New England, did not choose to
emigrate anywhere. But, having stoutly chosen to remain in America,
they had to decide, and immediately, on how best to pursue a viable
black American lifestyle. Some chose to accommodate, to placate the
American system by not antagonizing white readers with emphasis on
their blackness or abused lot. In some cases, writers scarcely
mentioned their blackness at all. If he had not been identified in the
lengthy title of his partial autobiography, it would be difficult to
distinguish Briton Hammon's slim volume from that of a narrative
told by a white servant of the times.[41]

Lemuel Haynes was born illegitimately in West Hartford, Connecticut, in 1753 of a black father and a New England white woman,
but, rejected by his parents, he was reared by a kindly couple to whom
he was indentured until he was ordained as a Congregationalist
minister in 1785. A Minuteman who served at Ticonderoga, he
married a respectable white woman and fathered nine children, all the
while preaching to all, or nearly all, white assemblies in western
Vermont, western Massachusetts, and upstate New York, all of this
without the slightest reported difficulty because of his race and color.
His biographer has published therein over three dozen of Haynes's
sermons—more were published elsewhere; a narrative of a topically
sensational mistaken murder conviction in Manchester,Vermont, in
1820; a brief, unfinished journal of a trip to Vermont; and more than
thirty-five of his letters, which date from 1795 through 1833, the year
of his death. Occasionally made aware of his color but, evidently,
never harried therefor, Haynes composed and delivered thousands
of religious discourses but nothing about the problems faced by most
blacks.[42]

William Stanley Braithwaite (1878–1962) has long been wrongly
regarded as one who accommodated the system and refused to write
anything black, but this is believed by those who have read only a
limited amount of his productions of over two dozen books. Two
volumes of his poetry, *Lyrics of Life and Love* (1904) and *The House*

of Falling Leaves (1908), are, pointedly, raceless. This "univer-
sality," however, is quite deliberate, for Braithwaite was anxious to
prove a literary point thereby, as he explained in a letter to black
novelist Nella Larsen:

> For twenty-five years I gave my best for the poets and poetry of
> America; it was a labor of love that cost me dearly; at the same
> time I proved something that no other man of the race dared even
> so much as attempt; I won something precious for the future
> hope and aspiration of the artistic and creative youth of
> America. . . .[43]

There were other early black New Englanders who were said, for
one reason or another, to have accommodated the prevailing American
mores, but most writers chose the route of open and defiant protest,
and usually in the name of blackness. Of these pieces, easily the most
sensational and, to whites, especially slaveholding whites, the most
frightening protest piece came from the fevered hand of Boston's
David Walker (1785–1830). A searing, uninhibited, and at times
uncontrolled jeremiad against American slavery and its proponents,
Walker's *Appeal, in Four Articles* . . . (1830) means to bare the fact
that "we Coloured People of these United States, are, the most
wretched and degraded and abject set of beings that ever lived since
the world began, and down to the present day, and, that the white
Christians . . . who hold us in slavery . . . treat us more cruel and
barbarous than any Heathen nation did any people whom it sub-
jected. . . ." Distributed surreptitiously throughout the slaveholding
South, where it was construed to be an appeal for mass insurrections
by slaves, the pamphlet provoked the circulation of rewards of $1,000
for Walker dead, and $10,000 for Walker alive. Walker nowhere in
his booklet seriously urged organized slavery insurrection, as has
been charged, but he did generously sprinkle his pages with menacing
statements, all of which were the easily misunderstood cries and
bravado of a desperately frustrated black man: "As true as the sun
ever shone . . . my color will root some of them out of the very face of
the earth. They shall have enough of making slaves of, and murdering
us. . . ." "Whites know well if we are men and see them mistreating us
in the manner they do, that there can be nothing in our hearts but death
alone for them; . . . whites may do their level best to enslave blacks, but
God will deliver us from you. And wo, wo will be to you if we have to

obtain our freedom by fighting. . . ." His death has long been a matter
of unsettled debate, some arguing that he was murdered by hired
assassins, others claiming he died otherwise. Utterly outraged at the
ravages of American slavery and prejudice, and almost chokingly
disgusted with black American passivity, Walker felt compelled to
write and publish his scorching booklet of eighty-eight pages, knowing
full well that by so doing, he might be abused or even murdered:

> If any are anxious to ascertain who I am, know the world, that I
> am one of the oppressed, degraded and wretched sons of
> Africa. . . . If any wish to plunge me into the wretched incapacity
> of a slave, or murder me for the truth, know ye, that I am in the
> hand of God, and at your disposal. I count my life not dear to me,
> but I am ready to be offered at any moment. . . .[44]

He has been called "the greatest living symbol of the protest
tradition during the 1880s and the early 1890s." He spent the first
nineteen years of his life as a Maryland slave, but, escaping to a
racially qualified freedom in New Bedford in 1838, where he lived for
ten years, Frederick Douglass (1817–1895) spent the rest of his long
life agitating, lecturing, writing against a whole spectrum of civil
wrongs suffered by his fellow blacks. A fairly steadfast adherent to the
theory of the American Melting Pot, although he did waver at least
once and almost defected to join blacks emigrating to Haiti,[45]
Douglass was one of the most memorable of all New England
Antislavery speakers. Of commanding eloquence and an accomplished writer, he wrote three autobiographies, a short story, uncounted dozens of addresses and speeches, and hundreds of letters,
not to mention columns in three newspapers he edited. Almost any
excerpt from any of his addresses might typify the man's massive
common sense and direct style, but an excerpt from an 1857 speech
remains popular to this day and can be seen on college campus posters
across the country:

> The whole history of the progress of human liberty shows that all
> concessions made to her august claims have been born of earnest
> struggle. . . . If there is no struggle there is no progress. Those
> who profess to favor freedom and yet deprecate agitation are
> men who want crops without plowing up the ground; they want
> rain without thunder and lightning. They want the ocean without
> the awful roar of its many waters. . . . Power concedes nothing
> without a demand. It never did and it never will. . . . [46]

Another early black New Englander in the protest tradition would be W. E. B. DuBois (1868–1963), born and reared in placid Great Barrington, Massachusetts. However, DuBois's genuine protest and propaganda became marked only later, during and beyond the time of the Harlem Renaissance. Always a prolific writer—he had produced almost forty books and pamphlets and hundreds of articles and introductions and reviews by 1924—his earlier, pre-renaissance writings were mostly "scientific" pieces written when he naively believed that white America needed only to become aware of the scientifically determined facts before it could properly think of the black man. Shocked by the persistence and blatant compounding of racism despite his display of scientific work, DuBois soon woke up, abandoned that tack, and took to unabashed propaganda. He could write in 1926, for instance, "all art is propaganda and ever must be, despite the wailings of the purists. . . . Whatever art I have for writing has been used always for propaganda. . . . I do not care a damn about art that is not propaganda. . . ."[47] But this view was expressive of a time beyond the limits of the earlier black New England writings.

By the end of the nineteenth century, all of New England could look back on measurable civil, political, and economic gains for the area's blacks. The birthings of these gains were midwifed into precarious being in no small, if historically unacknowledged, way by the kinds of literature here only glimpsed. Clearly, much of this literature is badly, emotionally, sentimentally, ungrammatically written and, were it not for the peculiarly extenuating circumstances, a lot of it might quickly be relegated to merciful oblivion. But, well written, as much of it also is, or rendered otherwise, this literature has unique worth. Writing on the backgrounds of colonial American literature, Kenneth Murdock has said:

> Even in the less artistically successful pages . . . there are usually
> other values no less real than the aesthetic. If a literature is the
> expression of the mind and emotions of a community, a record of
> its ideas, our definition of literary value must be broad enough to
> include not only artistic masterpieces but other documents
> which show what we as a people have and have not thought. . . .[48]

And by variously documenting the moral, political, psychological, and spiritual landscape of an otherwise overlooked, invisible America, this literature asserts its claims on living readers. If there be a preponderance of informative over aesthetic literature, it is largely so because these writers felt compelled to literally write themselves and their people into a visible, acceptable selfhood, into a viable Black I Am; and if the literature of knowledge, or propaganda, be the means by which that selfhood be wrenched from the grasp of the American creed of personal freedom and equality, then the literature of knowledge would serve, and did serve.

NOTES

1. Joe L. Davis, John T. Frederick, and Frank L. Mott, eds., *American Literature: An Anthology and Critical Survey*, 2 vols. (New York: Charles Scribner's Sons, 1948), I, 913, 918.

2. Edwin H. Cady, Frederick J. Hoffman, and Ray H. Pearce, eds., *The Growth of American Literature: A Critical and Historical Survey*, 2 vols. (New York: American Book Company, 1956), I, 9–12, 706–11.

3. Robert Bone, *The Negro Novel in America* (New Haven: Yale Univ. Press, 1958), pp. 236–38.

4. Robert Bone, *Down Home: A History of Afro-American Short Fiction from Its Beginnings to the End of the Harlem Renaissance* (New York: G. P. Putnam's Sons, 1979), p. 309.

5. William Wells Brown, *The Escape; or, A Leap for Freedom. A Drama, in Five Acts* (Boston: R. F. Wallcut, 1858).

6. William Wells Brown, *Experience; or, How to Give a Northern Man a Backbone*, in William E. Farrison, *William Wells Brown, Author and Reformer* (Chicago: Univ. of Chicago Press, 1969), p. 278. This play was also titled "The Doughface Baked; or, How to Get a Backbone," in *The National Anti-Slavery Standard* (19 April 1856); see Curtiss W. Ellison and E. W. Metcalf, *William Wells Brown and Martin R. Delany: A Reference Guide* (Boston: G. K. Hall and Co., 1978), p. 72.

7. Herbert Marshall and Mildred Strock, *Ira Aldridge: The Negro Tragedian* (Carbondale: Southern Illinois Univ. Press, 1958), p. 36.

8. Howard G. Belcher, "Mr. Tambo and Mr. Bones," *Rhode Island History*, 8, No. 4 (October 1969), 97–105.

9. Joan Sherman, *Invisible Poets: Afro-American Poets of the Nineteenth Century* (Urbana: Univ. of Illinois Press, 1976), p. vii.

10. Herbert Aptheker, *A Documentary History of the Negro People in the United States* (New York: Citadel Press, 1957), *passim*.

11. William Still, *The Underground Railroad* (Philadelphia: Porter & Coates, 1872), p. 275.

12. Still, p. 259.

13. Carter G. Woodson, ed., *The Mind of the Negro as Reflected in Letters Written During the Crisis 1800–1860* (Washington, D.C.: The Association for the Study of Negro Life and History, 1926), *passim*.

14. Sheldon H. Harris, *Paul Cuffe: Black America and the African Return* (New York: Simon and Schuster, 1972), pp. 159–265.

15. Dorothy Sterling, *Speak Out in Thunder Tones* (Garden City: Doubleday & Company, Inc., 1973), pp. 39–42.

16. Timothy M. Cooley, *Sketches of the Life and Character of the Rev. Lemuel Haynes, A.M.* (New York: John S. Taylor, 1839), pp. 93–76.

17. Harris, pp. 77–158.

18. Ray Allen Billington, ed., *The Journal of Charlotte L. Forten* (New York: The Dryden Press, 1953), p. 31.

19. William H. Robinson, ed., *The Proceedings of the Free African Union Society & The African Benevolent Society* (Providence: The Urban League of Rhode Island, 1976), *passim*.

20. Charles Nichols, *Many Thousand Gone: The Ex-Slaves' Account of Their Bondage and Freedom* (Bloomington: Indiana Univ. Press, 1963), p. xiii.

21. James Mars, *The Life of James Mars, A Slave Born and Sold in Connecticut. Written by Himself* (Hartford: Press of Case, Lockwood & Company, 1864) in Arna Bontemps, ed., *Five Black Lives* (Middletown: Wesleyan Univ. Press, 1971), pp. 35–58. An 11th edition appeared as late as 1872.

22. William Grimes, *Life of William Grimes, the Runaway Slave, Brought down to the Present Time. Written by Himself* (New Haven: By the Author, 1835), in Arna Bontemps, ed., *Five Black Lives* (Middletown: Wesleyan Univ. Press, 1971), pp. 59–128. This is an enlargement of an 1825 edition published in New York.

23. Moses Grandy, *Narrative of the Life of Moses Grandy, late a Slave in the United States*, 2nd edition (Boston, 1844), 44 pp., in William L. Katz, ed., *Five Slave Narratives* (New York: Arno Press/New York Times, 1960), unpaginated.

24. Jacob Stroyer, *Sketches of My Life in the South. Part 1*, 4th edition (Salem, 1897), 100 pp., in William L. Katz, ed., *Five Slave Narratives* (New York: Arno Press/New York Times, 1960), unpaginated.

25. William J. Brown, *The Life of William J. Brown of Providence, R.I. With Personal Recollections of Incidents in Rhode Island* (Providence: Angell & Co., 1883), 230 pp.

26. Nancy Prince, *A Narrative of the Life and Times and Travels of Mrs. Nancy Prince. Written by Herself*, 3rd edition (Boston: By the Author, 1856), p. i.

27. Carter G. Woodson, ed., *Negro Orators and Their Orations* (Washington, D.C.: The Association for the Study of Negro Life and History, 1925), *passim*.

28. Philip S. Foner, ed., *The Life and Writings of Frederick Douglass*, 5 vols. (New York: The International Publishers, 1950–1975), *passim*.

29. Philip S. Foner, ed., *The Voice of Black America: Major Speeches by Negroes in the United States 1797–1971* (New York: Simon and Schuster, 1972), *passim*.

30. Prince Hall, *Charge Delivered to the Brethren of the African Lodge, on the Twenty-Fifth of June, 1792, in Charleston* (Boston, 1792), 6 pp.

31. William Wells Brown, *A Lecture Delivered Before the Female Anti-Slavery Society of Salem, Lyceum Hall, Nov. 14, 1847 . . . Reported by Henry M. Parkhurst, Phonographic Reporter, Boston* (Boston: Massachusetts Antislavery Society, 1847).

32. Anon., *Address Delivered to the Alumni at Harvard University, June 24, 1896, After Receiving the Honorary Master of Arts* (Boston, 1896), 4 pp.

33. [Prince Hall?], *A Sermon [preached to the Prince Hall African Masonic Lodge, No. 459, Boston] By the Rev. Bro. John Marrant, Chaplain. ROMANS XII., 10* (Boston, 1784), 16 pp.

34. Maria W. Stewart, *Productions of Mrs. Maria W. Stewart, Presented to the First African Baptist Society, of the City of Boston* (Boston: Friends of Freedom and Virtue, 1835).

35. Maria W. Stewart, *Meditations from the Pen of Mrs. Maria W. Stewart, Negro* (Washington, D. C., 1879).

36. Pauline Hopkins, *Contending Forces: A Romance Illustrative of Negro Life, North and South* (Boston: The Colored Co-Operative Publishing Company, 1900).

37. J. P. Mayer, ed., *Alexis De Tocqueville: Democracy in America*, trans. by George Lawrence (Garden City: Doubleday & Company, Inc., 1969), p. 364.

38. Robinson, pp. 24–25.

39. Sherman, pp. 42–52.

40. James T. Holly, *A Vindication of the Capacity of the Negro Race for Self-Government and Civilized Progress as Demonstrated by Historical Events of the Haitian Revolution* (New Haven: Afric-American Printing Co., 1857), p. 45.

41. Briton Hammon, *A Narrative of the Uncommon Sufferings, and Surprizing Deliverance of Briton Hammon, a Negro Man, Servant to General Winslow of*

Marshfield, in New England; Who returned to Boston, after having been absent almost thirteen years (Boston: Green and Russell, 1760).

42. Cooley, *passim*.

43. Philip Butcher, ed., *The William Stanley Braithwaite Reader* (Ann Arbor: Univ. of Michigan Press, 1972), p. 284.

44. David Walker, *Walker's Appeal in Four Articles. Third and Last edition, with additional Notes, Corrections &c.* (Boston: By the Author, 1830), p. 79.

45. Floyd J. Miller, *The Search for a Black Nationality, Black Emigration and Colonization 1787–1853* (Urbana: Univ. of Illinois Press, 1975), pp. 239–40.

46. *The Life and Writings of Frederick Douglass*, pp. 11, 437.

47. Julius Lester, ed., *The Seventh Son. The Thought and Writing of W. E. B. DuBois*, 2 vols. (New York: Random House, 1971), II, 319.

48. Kenneth Murdock, "The Colonial and Revolutionary Period," in Arthur H. Quinn, ed., *The Literature of the American People: An Historical and Critical Survey* (New York: Appleton, Century, Crofts, Inc., 1954), p. 4.

210754

New England and the Invention of the South

Leslie Fiedler

On a bare northern summit
A pine-tree stands alone.
He slumbers; and around him
The icy snows are blown.

His dreams are of a palm-tree
Who in far lands of morn
Amid the blazing desert
Grieves silent and forlorn.

Ein Fichtenbaum steht einsam
Heinrich Heine

Everyone knows that the image of American slavery and the ante-bellum South was created not by slow accretion, but all at once, overnight, as it were, by a single mid-nineteenth-century book, Harriet Beecher Stowe's *Uncle Tom's Cabin.* Translated from language to language and medium to medium (first to the stage, then the movies, comic books, T.V.) it created not just certain mythological Black characters, Uncle Tom, Eliza, Topsy, but the mythic landscape through which they still move in the dream of America dreamed by native Americans as well as by Europeans, Africans, and Asians of all ages and all degrees of sophistication.

Mrs. Stowe was not the first American author to have created Negro characters. They had appeared earlier in novels and stories by such eminent writers as James Fenimore Cooper, Edgar Allan Poe, and Herman Melville; but somehow they had remained archetypally

101

inert, refusing to leap from the printed page to the public domain. And though the long-lived Minstrel Show (which still survives on British T.V.) had begun to invent its pervasive stereotypes of plantation life before Mrs. Stowe ever set pen to paper, they, too, failed to kindle the imagination of the world. To be sure, Mrs. Stowe herself was influenced by them; so that before we learn the real name of George and Eliza Harris' small son, Harry, we hear him hailed as "Jim Crow." Many of the minor darkies who surround her serious protagonists are modelled on the clowns in blackface who cracked jokes with a White Interlocutor.

But clearly images of Black Americans could not stir an emotional response adequate to the horrors of slavery so long as they remained merely comic. Small wonder then that Mr. Bones retreated to the wings once Eliza had fled the bloodhounds on the ice (only in the dramatic version, to be sure) and Uncle Tom had been beaten to death in full view of a weeping house. Nor is it surprising that the figure of the martyred Black slave under the lash, too old to be a sexual threat, too pious to evoke fears of violent revenge, captured the deep fantasy of a White world, haunted (since the Haitian revolt at least) with nightmares of Black Insurrection, and needing, therefore, to be assured that tears rather than blood would be sufficient to erase their guilt.

What is puzzling (though somehow few critics have paused long enough to puzzle it out) is that Uncle Tom was the creation not of some son of the South, a literate Black runaway slave, perhaps, or a tormented Byronic White Planter, like Mrs. Stowe's Augustine St. Clare, but of a daughter of New England, who seemed fated by nature and nurture to become the laureate of that region rather than of a Southland she scarcely knew. It was, indeed, as a New England local-colorist that she began and ended her literary career. Her first published story and her first published book were set in that icy and rockbound world, and her final works were genre studies, evoking scenes of her own Connecticut childhood and that of her husband, who had grown up in Maine. Yet no matter how hard hightone critics, who distrust the sentimentality and egregious melodrama of her most popular novel, may tout them, ordinary readers do not remember her for *The Minister's Wooing* or *Old Town Folks*.

What such readers, what I myself, prize her for constitutes in effect an interruption, a detour in her career: a temporary abandonment of her essential subject matter, which was in any case domestic rather than political. Indeed, the sole public issue which ever engaged her as a writer was Slavery, to which she devoted some five or six years of her life, producing finally three books: *Uncle Tom's Cabin* (1852), *The Key to Uncle Tom's Cabin* (1853), and *Dred: A Tale of the Dismal Swamp* (1856), of which only the first is still read with pleasure. After the failure of the last, she abandoned slavery as a fictional theme forever, returning to the South only to sing, in *Palmetto-Leaves* (1873), praises to Florida as a tourist refuge from the rigors of the New England Winter.

But much earlier she had begun to be aware of the South in a way she would never have been if she had never left home—never followed her father to Cincinnati, where she lived for eighteen crucial years of her life between her twenty-first and thirty-ninth birthday. It was there she married Calvin Stowe, there she bore her first six children, losing one in infancy. To be sure Cincinnati thought of itself as a Western rather than a Southern city; but it bordered on the upper South, separated only by the width of the Ohio River from Kentucky, where the action of Mrs. Stowe's immortal novel begins. It was, moreover, a place where Slaves and ex-Slaves were highly visible: on the one hand, a stop on the Underground Railway; on the other, a city of Black-White Conflict, of riot and murder, of rape and rumors of rape. Harriet was, however, somewhat removed from all that, living as she did in the Lane Seminary, a kind of New England missionary enclave, for which slavery was less a fact of daily existence than an occasion for theological debate and schism.

She did not, in any event, write *Uncle Tom's Cabin* in Cincinnati, *could* not write it—or even dream it—until she returned to her native New England, following, or rather preceding her husband, who had been offered a job at Bowdoin College in Brunswick, Maine. Some twenty-five or thirty years before, he had been a student at that unredeemably rural and ferociously Calvinist school, a poor boy then fighting to rise in the world by sheer intellect and energy, a professor of moral theology now and married to one of the aristocratic Beechers. He seems not to have been very happy at his job, however, not finding among his students, perhaps, any to equal those of his own time, who included not just a future president of the United States, Franklin Pierce, but Nathaniel Hawthorne and Henry Wadsworth Longfellow; which is to say, two men who between them created (think of Hester

Prynne and her "steeple-crowned" persecutors, of Miles Standish, John and Priscilla Alden) figures as essential to the myth of New England as Uncle Tom, Simon Legree, and Little Eva to the myth of the South.

But it was not of Bowdoin that Harriet wrote even after the child with which she was pregnant on her trip from Ohio had been delivered and she had settled down to writing for popular magazines again in her endless effort to catch up with the household bills. That college, it seemed, was doomed never to be memorialized in literature for all the gifted writers who had inhabited its halls. Hawthorne, it is true, had tried in his first novel, *Fanshawe*, to describe the solitude of its setting: "secluded from the sight and sound of the busy world . . . almost at the farthest extremity of a narrow vale . . . as inaccessible, except at one point, as the Happy Valley of Abyssinia"; but he had suppressed that book immediately after publication. Nor was Mrs. Stowe tempted to emulate him, since in everything she wrote she was more concerned with the spaces inside which men and women live than those through which they move. Moreover, when she did turn her attention outward from houses and furnished rooms, she was more likely to deal with imaginary landscapes than real ones.

In any case, finding herself in a region further northeast than she had ever been before, a kind of ultimate, absolute New England, evoked in her images of ultimate, absolute South: a mythic Louisiana and Mississippi, in which Black field hands and White overseers toiled in cottonfields under a sweltering sun. But she remained unaware of this for many months. At first, indeed, as December storms shook the house around her and she lay sleepless beside her half-frozen babies, she thought instead of the blizzards of her childhood, her parents struggling homeward through mounting drifts. But seated at a Communion Service in the college church of Bowdoin in February of 1852, she saw before her, lit by a meridional glare brighter than the dim northern light at the windows, the bloody and broken body of an old Black man beaten to death by his White master. And barely repressing her tears, she rushed home to write down (the words are her son's, remembering, echoing hers years afterward) "the vision which had been blown into her mind as by a mighty wind."

Then, the ink scarcely dry, she read the first installment of what was to become *Uncle Tom's Cabin* aloud to her children, who "broke into convulsions of weeping," and only when they were asleep did she permit herself to give way to tears. "I remember," she wrote to one of her sons a quarter of a century later, "weeping over you as you lay sleeping beside me, and I thought of the slave mothers whose babies were torn from them." But surely she was thinking, too, of the child she had lost before leaving Cincinnati: the son she always referred to as "the most beautiful and beloved" of all her brood, since elsewhere—indeed, more than once—she noted for posterity that "it was at his dying bed that I learned what a poor slave mother may feel when her child is torn away from her. . . ." And she added, "I felt that I could never be consoled for it, unless this crushing of my own heart might enable me to work out some great good to others. . . ."

The "great good" turned out to be, of course, *Uncle Tom's Cabin*, whose serial publication she began almost immediately, not quite knowing at first where she was going or how long it would take her but sustained, it would appear, by other hallucinations as vivid as the first, so that finally she began to believe her book had been *given* from without (by God, she liked to say) rather than invented from within. Yet the essential feeling of the book is that of a bereaved White mother, a kind of latter-day Rachel who weeps for her children and will not be comforted. Very early on in that book she appeals, in fact, to others who, like her, have suffered the loss of a child, as the kindly little Mrs. Bird prepares to give the clothing of her dead son to Eliza's Harry: "And oh! mother that reads this, has there never been in your house a drawer, or a closet, the opening of which has been to you like the opening again of a little grave?" Indeed, Eliza seems in many ways an apter surrogate for Mrs. Stowe than Uncle Tom, being introduced in a chapter called simply "The Mother." Yet though Eliza is threatened with the loss of Harry, she never actually is deprived of him even for a moment, so that we tend to forget the babe in her arms, remembering her not as "The Mother" but as the Fleeing Maiden, an object of inter-racial lust, like Cissy and Emmeline at the book's conclusion.

There are, to be sure, in the chapters between, many Black mothers deprived of their children by slave-traders and driven in despair to drink or self-inflicted death. But somehow the scenes that involve them, though pathetic enough, lack the mythic resonance of the death of Uncle Tom, with which it all began, or even that of Little Eva, which rivalled it in popularity, at least on the boards. Both

scenes, of course, provide opportunities for a "good cry," but more
than that they have similar theological meanings: the pearl-pale,
golden-haired, barely-pubescent virgin becoming, like the wooly-
headed old Black at the moment of death, a secular avatar of Christ.
Both die, that is to say, for our sins, the sins of slavery and blind lust
and contempt for the bourgeois family.

But interestingly enough in light of Mrs. Stowe's own deep self-
consciousness, there is no mourning Mary figure present at Eva's
death, no bereaved mother to weep as Mrs. Stowe had wept. Mrs. St.
Clare, who bore Eva, is an anti-Mother: a vain, silly, cruel,
hypochondriacal woman, a fading beauty, who loves and pities no one
but herself. If she is called "Marie" it is to emphasize the irony of her
relationship to the Christ-like child she has borne and lost without
ever knowing it. In any case, Eva's death-bed scene is presided over
by her Byronic father and Uncle Tom, who must sustain him, too, in
his grief, as if he were another child. It is a strange kind of Protestant
Pietà that Mrs. Stowe portrays: a Daughter, a Father, and a Slave.
But no mother. Or is it that Tom is revealed in that scene as the
symbolic, archetypal, mythological Mother he has really been all
along?

It would seem, indeed, that for Mrs. Stowe (and this provides the
link between the passion that begot her book and the image in which it
became incarnate) Woman=Mother=Slave=Black; or simplifying,
Woman=Black, Black=Woman. Perhaps the final formulation most
accurately represents Mrs. Stowe's perception of the relationship
between race and gender, since, unlike certain hardcore feminists of
her time and ours, she was far from believing that women played the
role *vis à vis* men of "niggers." Yet Charlotte Bronte seems to have
thought so, or at least this is the way Ellen Moers would interpret her
comment that "Mrs. Stowe had felt the iron of slavery enter into her
heart, from childhood upwards. . . ."

It seems to me, however, that Mrs. Stowe, being what we would
now call a "sexist" as well as a "racist," believed that just as males
and females were intrinsically different, so also were Whites and
Blacks, and that, moreover, their differences corresponded exactly,
i.e., "the Anglo-Saxon race" possessed those qualities considered in
Mrs. Stowe's age "masculine," being "stern, inflexible, energetic . . .
dominant and commanding," at their worst, "hot and hasty."
"Africans," on the other hand, were—like women as Mrs. Stowe
understood them—"naturally patient, timid and unenterprising, not

naturally daring . . . but home-loving and affectionate. . . ." And Tom, being the most African of all (as opposed, say, to George Harrison, a mulatto with certain *macho* traits inherited from his White father), is the most womanly, most motherly, possessing "to the full, the gentle domestic heart which, woe for them, is characteristic of his unhappy race."

If we understand the sense in which Tom is a White Mother in Blackface, we realize that when Mrs. Stowe sighs "woe for them" she means also "woe for us": we long-suffering, pious WASP mothers, daughters, and wives, who respond to the indignities visited upon us with forgiveness and prayer, as is appropriate to *our* "gentle, domestic hearts." There is, then, a sense in which Mrs. Stowe's novel, despite the fact that she rejected radical feminism, even as she rejected radical abolitionism, is—just below its surface—a protest on behalf of women as well as of slaves. In this sense surely she is true to the New England culture, which not only produced certain pioneers of Feminism, real and fictional, like Margaret Fuller and Hester Prynne, but in Harriet's time was characterized by a progressive movement which advocated simultaneously Rights for Women, Freedom for Slaves, and the Prohibition of Whiskey, a third major theme of her complexly didactic romance.

It was, I am suggesting, fitting (perhaps even inevitable) that a crusading woman, daughter, and sister to crusading clerics end by mythicizing slavery as an offense not just against the teachings of Christ but more immediately against the bourgeois family and that in the course of doing so she create archetypal images of their owners as well as the dark and lovely land in which flourished what Mrs. Stowe called—with multiple ironies that escaped her control—the "patri-archal institution." But she did not do so, could not do so, until the passing of the Fugitive Slave Law had made manifest the complicity of Massachusetts and Connecticut and Maine in that institution so that it was no longer possible to attribute the guilt of treating humans with Black skins as things solely to alien others in the alien South.

This became especially clear when in the midst of Mrs. Stowe's trek from Cincinnati to Brunswick, on March 7, 1850, Daniel Webster, spokesman for, living embodiment of, the political con-science of New England publicly defended that atrocious law. At that point what had been an inter-sectional conflict became a family quarrel. "So fallen! so lost! the light withdrawn/ Which once he wore!" Whittier wrote of that failed brother, more in sadness than anger, "The glory from his gray hairs gone/ Forevermore!" And at almost the same moment, Mrs. Stowe's sister-in-law was pleading in a letter, "Now, Hattie, if I could use a pen as you can, I would write something that would make this whole nation feel what an accursed thing slavery is."

If this sequence of events does not make it clear, the text of *Uncle Tom's Cabin* does, that when Harriet began to turn her vision into words she was concerned not only with how "accursed" the "patriarchal institution" was, but also—and perhaps most of all—with how ignominious was the moral capitulation before its claims of her own beloved New England. Simon Legree, the chief villain of her novel, is, as everyone knows, not a Southern planter, overseer, or trader, but a Vermonter, the faithless son of a saintly New England mother much like what Harriet believed her own son to be, who in a decaying plantation house bereft of white women presides over the murder of a nonresisting Black male while pursuing in drunken lust helpless Black females. And surely Legree was also an actor in Mrs. Stowe's original vision; if not the actual killer (it is unclear what his color was in the first instance; in the book he is split in two and made Black), then the shadowy Third Man, who *was* White from the start and who urged the murderer on, an accomplice before and after the fact.

In any event, it seems to me that both Tom and Simon, the blessed "slave" who dies forgiving his enemies and the damned "master" who drags out his last days unable to forgive even himself, represent aspects of the pious, guilt-ridden, and hopelessly divided psyche of Harriet Beecher Stowe. Insofar as she is a woman, she identifies with the loving persecuted slave; insofar as she is a New Englander, she identifies with his brutal persecutor. It is worth recalling at this point that Mrs. Stowe's Grandmother Foote had two indentured Black servants, who, though they could look forward to eventual freedom, were obliged to call their mistress's grand-daughter "Miss Harriet" while to her they were simply Harry and Dinah. That that experience stayed with her we know from the fact that the first named Black character in her book, the threatened Black child of Eliza, is called "Harry" while the cook in the kitchen of the St. Clare house is named "Dinah," though she resembles physically the woman who helped out with Mrs. Stowe's cooking in Cincinnati, "a regular epitome of slave life in herself, fat, gentle, easy, loving and loveable," who, to complicate matters even further, was named Eliza.

Almost all of Harriet's real, close relations with Black people were as a Mistress (however enlightened and benevolent) dealing with servants. That this was a troubling fact one would never gather from her letters on the subject; but when in her novel she attempts to portray ideal or utopian families, they turn out to be *servantless*: like the orderly Vermont home from which Miss Ophelia comes, where the Lady of the house has cleaned and arranged and provided long before anyone else has arisen or the Quaker Household of Rachel Halliday, in which adults and children in peaceful concert handle all the chores. No servants, Black or White, and, I cannot resist adding at this point, no resident Blacks at all, since Mrs. Stowe cannot imagine a world in which Black and White inhabit the same country in peace, much less cohabit and beget in a bi-racial family. Symptomatically, then, at the end of her book, all the major Black characters who are not dead are on their way to Liberia. In Mrs. Stowe's quite un-utopian households (she was a notoriously disorganized housekeeper) what order was maintained was maintained by servants, a large part of them Black, and the difficulties this caused her, as well as the guilt it bred, can best be understood by looking closely at Miss Ophelia's adventures in New Orleans.

Though Mrs. Stowe believed in repatriating Black Americans, she did not propose to send them back to Africa until they had been educated and converted by White Americans like her, i.e., turned into literate missionaries who would eventually Christianize all of the continent from which they had been so cruelly snatched. Indeed, since she herself had been a teacher before she became a housewife, Mrs. Stowe had known Black people, particularly small children, as students earlier than as servants, and she represents the pathos and comedy (as well as the underlying terror) of her attempts to deal with what sometimes must have seemed their invincible ignorance in the encounters between Miss Ophelia and Topsy. But the figure of Miss Ophelia is more complex and important than that. The only other New Englander besides Legree who is close to, if not quite at the mythic center of the novel, she is clearly another projection of or surrogate for the author as New Englander.

We must not be misled by the superficial differences between this bristling, cold, compulsively orderly Old Maid and the warm-hearted, hopelessly untidy mother of seven who conceived her. She represents a caricature, drawn not without a certain degree of self-hatred, of Harriet Beecher Stowe as do-gooder, meddler in the affairs of others, impotent voyeur. Perpetually outside of everything, essentially unable to communicate with anyone or influence anything (who can really believe in the eventual redemption of Topsy?), Miss Ophelia stands in a particularly absurd relationship to Black slavery since despite her abstract conviction that slaves are fully human, she cannot bear to touch their flesh. Even more equivocal and suspect is her relationship to Southern culture, whose slovenliness, leisurely pace, and sensuality she affects to despise, though secretly she is titillated by its beauty, envious of its easy charm. Finally she is, like the rugged landscape of Maine, like Mrs. Stowe (who always deprecated her own looks), like New England piety itself, perhaps, without beauty and without charm but not without guilt, despite her high ideals and blameless life.

To understand the source of that guilt in her and her author, I propose to return once more to Mrs. Stowe's Bowdoin "vision," explicating yet another level of its meaning with the aid of an essay by Sigmund Freud, which actually mentions *Uncle Tom's Cabin* and is called "A Child is Being Beaten." In it Freud discusses a fantasy which he kept encountering in cases of pathological sado-masochism (a fantasy disconcertingly like one central to many popular books of the nineteenth century, most particularly perhaps Dickens' *Oliver Twist* and *David Copperfield*) in which a small boy or girl is being brutally whipped. As far as literature is concerned, almost any helpless or relatively powerless victim will do as well: a horse, a dog, an abused wife, a Black Slave; all that is absolutely necessary is a whip, a half-visible wielder, and a victim who does not or cannot resist. It is a multi-purpose symbol signifying social injustice and perverse pleasure, and it can stir therefore guilt and self-righteousness, tears and sexual excitement. No wonder it has been exploited to make best-sellers and to fuel social reform—in *Uncle Tom's Cabin* both at once.

But, I am tempted to ask at this point (and here Freud does not finally help), with whom does the fantasizer of such scenes, with whom did Mrs. Stowe, identify, the beater, or the beaten? Though my first impulse was to say with the beaten, the child, the wife, the slave, the Black—helpless, perhaps, but not guiltless nor wholly sympathetic until beaten to the verge of death or beyond, my second was to say also the beater: the parent, the husband, the master/mistress, the White—guilty without a doubt, but also a victim, powerless to compel submission or to stay his/her own fury. The fantasizer identifies with both then, *both*, and feels guilty on both counts: guilty enough to have been punished in the first instance (and who, Mrs. Stowe's theology asked, is without sin?), but guilty in the last of having dared to punish (vengeance is mine, says Mrs. Stowe's patriarchal God) the offending other. Even this is not the whole truth, however, since—as the figure of Miss Ophelia suggests—the sado-masochistic fantasizer is not just beater, he is also something, someone else: an onlooker, a third party who watches both the sufferer and the inflictor of suffering, finding double pleasure in being, though vicariously both, in fact neither.

But Miss Ophelia is our surrogate in the novel as well as Mrs. Stowe's since we watch what she watches, watch through her, as it were. And this eye-to-the-keyhole effect, this observing at a double remove what is too obscene to be observed firsthand, much less done, constitutes the very essense of pornography. Moreover, the sneaky pleasure it affords us is compounded by the pretense of piety which writers like Mrs. Stowe afford us: a claim that we are looking at such ultimate atrocities even as she is showing them, only in order to bear witness, to protest, maybe to change it all for the better. I have always experienced, in any case, the same sickening revulsion/attraction in reading *Uncle Tom's Cabin* that I do, for instance, watching the films on child-abuse whose current popularity on T.V. must be explicable, in part at least, because they provide us with vicarious opportunities to relish the maceration of children's flesh while pretending to deplore it—or rather, *really* deploring it.

Nor am I alone in my response to Mrs. Stowe's all-time bestseller, which has been read, it seems ironical in this context to remind you, with equal pleasure in the kitchen, the parlor, and the nursery. Similar opinions have been expressed by writers as different from each other and me as that Black child of Harlem, James Baldwin, and that White daughter of the early twentieth-century South, Margaret Mitchell, whose belated fictional response to Mrs. Stowe's improbable master-piece has rivalled it in sales. Baldwin speaks of "the ostentatious parading of excessive and spurious emotion," which he calls "the mask of cruelty," while Mrs. Mitchell, through the mouth of Scarlett O'Hara, refers contemptuously to the "nasty and illbred interest" of Mrs. Stowe and her first Northern female fans in "branding irons, cat-of-ninetails and slave concubinage." Small wonder, then, that some of Freud's sado-masochistic patients, in an attempt to revive and refresh their own flagging fantasies, would while masturbating to climax read that pious and sentimental piece of New England porn.

In any case, we cannot begin to understand *Uncle Tom's Cabin* (as I am always beginning again to understand it in an essentially endless quest) unless we are aware that, gifted with easy access to her own unconscious and trained by her Calvinist forebears in conscious self-examination, Mrs. Stowe was able to draw a triple portrait of her guilt-ridden self at the very heart of her sentimental, didactic bestseller. As a bereaved White Mother, she identified with a victimized and forgiving Black male. As a Beecher, her father's truest heir and, in that sense, a betrayer of her mother, she portrayed herself as an iron-muscled White male, a murderer and rapist. As her sister's sister, another frustrated New England schoolmarm and reformer, she projected herself in the half-comic figure of a prurient do-gooder, a spinster with no home of her own.

But what began as a private fantasy disguised, even from herself, as a popular protest novel ("Everybody's protest novel," Baldwin called it with loving bitterness) has become a national myth: a perceptual grid through which we continue to perceive slavery, abolition, and the ante-bellum South, indeed, our whole country and culture. But this is to say that finally *Uncle Tom's Cabin* is a social, a cultural, fact, quite as real as public documents like the Fugitive Slave Law or the Emancipation Proclamation and one, moreover, still read rather than merely read about.

Literary Boston:
The Change of Taste
at the End of the Century

Martin Green

I would like to take for granted a double proposition: that between 1830 and 1880 Boston had an ambitious appetite for the products of high culture; and that by 1900 that was no longer true—that by then, especially if we concentrate on the fine arts, conservative Boston clearly dominated the other elements in the city; so that it comes as no surprise that, for instance, the Armoury Show should have been held in New York and not here. I want to take that for granted, and to concentrate on what we *can* see in that decline and declivity of art, that valley of taste, what there was that was yet active, positive, growing. I make no claims to completeness, but the phenomenon of that kind that strikes me is the taste for Kipling in Boston. But, as will become apparent, I have in mind something rather complicated; there are some quite disparate phenomena I am going to associate with Kipling, so I would like to refer to this more abstractly as an episode of Kiplingism.

In the early part of his career, Kipling was in love with America, and America reciprocated. He married an American and came to live in Vermont. He became in effect an American author; at the time of his death, his total sales were estimated at seven million volumes in England, eight million in America. He became one of America's myth-makers. In 1895 Theodore Roosevelt invited him to dine together with Owen Wister and Frederick Remington, who were collaborating on the stories and essays in which the cowboy myth was created for America. Indeed, Wister had been inspired to those efforts by a remark that America needed a Kipling of the sagebrush.

And even the men of conscience, the liberals and aesthetes of Boston, were attracted to Kipling in those years. Henry James wrote to his brother William on February 6, 1892, "Kipling strikes me personally as the most complete man of genius (as distinct from fine intelligence) that I have ever known."[1] James wrote an introduction to a collection of Kipling's stories, published in America in 1891, called *Mine Own People*. And on November 5, 1896, he wrote to Jonathan Sturges, about *Seven Seas*, "I am laid low by the absolutely uncanny talent—the prodigious special faculty of it. It's all *violent*, without a dream of nuance or a hint of 'distinction.' . . . But it's magnificent and masterly in its way, and full of the most insidious art."[2] And Charles Eliot Norton, writing in *The Atlantic Monthly* in 1892, said that Kipling "is one of those poets who have done England service in strengthening the foundations of her influence and of her fame."[3]

Lafcadio Hearn, writing in 1897, called Kipling "the greatest of all living English poets, greater than all before him in the line he has taken. As for England, he is her Saga-man—skald, scôp, whatever you like."[4] For Jack London and Frank Norris, he was the greatest inspiration as a prose writer and truth teller. "Oh who will be *our* Kipling?" Norris wrote, "Who will tell *our* stories?" For above all, Kipling seemed an Anglo-American phenomenon. The frontier humorists Mark Twain and Bret Harte had been his masters, and Walter Besant said that Kipling was the first writer in English to have a world audience of 100,000,000 Anglo-Saxons; Edmund Dowden said Kipling was the master of our tribal lays, so that any morsel of his verse constituted a historical event for two hemispheres.

W. D. Howells, writing in *McClure's Magazine*, March, 1897, claimed Kipling as an American poet. "He has, in fact, given us a kind of authority to do so by divining our actual average better than any American I can think of off-hand, in this very extraordinary poem, where he supposes the spirit of America to speak at a well-known moment of civic trouble." Here he quoted the whole of "An American." "There is no one else to name with him. He is, by virtue of his great gift, the laureate of that larger England whose wreath is not for any prime minister to bestow. . . ."[5] And we may come back finally to Norton and *The Atlantic Monthly*, that main voice of literary

Boston: "This splendid continuous fertility of English genius, this unbroken expression of English character and life from Chaucer to Rudyard Kipling, is unparalleled in the moral and intellectual history of any other race."[6]

And what does a taste for Kipling tell us about the rest of Boston's tastes and aptitudes? We are probably inclined to answer "imperialism." During the 1890s, Alfred Thayer Mahan was preaching imperialism (in very Kipling-like terms) to America; and *The Atlantic Monthly* was one of his principal pulpits; its editor, Horace Scudder, had especially invited him to deliver his message there. But we should remember that Norton, for instance, was nobly anti-imperialist in the crucial issue of the Spanish-American War. I would say that a taste for Kipling meant above all a sense of responsibility—but a sense, a phase, in which the pride was post-Puritan, marked with melancholy stoicism, and the energies of expansion were in some ways blighted by, in other ways stimulated by, a fear of debility and decay. That is, I think, the mood that Kipling served in Boston as elsewhere. But his art is peculiarly inaccessible to serious readers now, and we incline to dismiss the taste for him as mere vulgarity, which is unfair to him and to his readers. In fact, Kipling was profoundly innovative; no one's work could be called more of an antithesis to the Victorian style in art.

I have begun to use the slogan "The Blues of a Master Class" to give my students an idea of how to read Kipling, and I think one has to understand his role in Boston in some such terms. What I mean by blues is a sonorous ensemble of phrases, which evoke certain situations, presenting them as typical for a social group; so that by declaiming them, the singer unites the audience into a group identity—united implicitly in separation from other groups. When the situation is erotic, the group effect is of course indirect, but I think it is always there. The griefs or problems or misadventures named happen to "people like us." And though the declamation is plangent and potentially melancholy, it is also proud and self-affirming; the emotional coloring combines many shades, and it is up to the listener to respond according to his mood, his taste, his character.

Now Boston at the end of the century was of course a city full of the blues of the master class, and so ripe for Kiplingism. I feel I can say "of course" even if my readers don't agree, because I have advanced all my reasons for saying so in *The Problem of Boston*. But as an example, I would cite Robert Lowell's *Life-Studies* as a vivid depiction of a slice of Boston culture still having a strong sense of hereditary responsibility but at the same time thoroughly Kiplingized—the dominant imagery of responsibility by 1900 being adventure and the aristo-military caste.

Let me quote to you briefly from "91 Revere Street" in that volume. Lowell describes his father—and his naval friends—as follows. "His opinions were almost morbidly hesitant, but he considered himself a matter-of-fact man of science and had an unspoiled faith in the superior efficiency of northern nations. He modeled his allegiances and humor on the cockney imperialism of Rudyard Kipling's swearing Tommies, who did their job. Autochthonous Boston snobs . . . were alarmed by the brassy callousness of our naval visitors, who labeled the Italians they met on Revere Street as 'grade-A' and 'grade-B wops.' "[7] You see there three successive phases in the sensibility of ruling class Boston; the autochthonous snobs, with their loyalties to the responsible society of the nineteenth century; the Kipling episode embodied in Lowell's father, under the aegis of the English poet's images; and the modernist phase embodied in the twentieth-century poet, whose phrasing declares his alienation from both precursors equally.

It would be easy to connect Kipling's work in literature to the other arts of the time (for instance, to Sullivan and Elgar in music) and to show the antithesis and opposition between Kiplingism and the modernism that so quickly displaced it. T. S. Eliot was the Bostonian anti-Kipling figure in poetry for Lowell and his like, though Eliot later came to see Kipling as the greatest man of letters of his generation. That sort of argument is, I think, not problematic, and in fact I have done something of the sort in the Kipling chapter in *Dreams of Adventure, Deeds of Empire.*

But I have found it more profitable, in trying to bring people to see the point of Kipling, both in his own period and now, to say something about the blues—though I am no expert in that subject. However, that is all the more reason to explain what I mean by the phrase, which is that Afro-American vocal and instrumental style which goes with three-line lyrics, of which the first line is repeated, AAB, and with a slow plangent, declamatory rhythm, with falsetto breaks in the voice, and much room for improvisation by both singer and instrumentalist—essentially simple and folk-rooted in its message, but made complex and sophisticated by the music.

Historically speaking, W. C. Handy reported first hearing blues in the Mississippi Delta in 1895, when the field holler was adapted to guitar accompaniment. (This is of course just about the time when Kipling was making his biggest impact, and the coincidence is more than accidental.) Bessie Smith was the first famous vocalist, in the 1920s; most of the great vocalists were women, like Ma Rainey, though the instrumentalists were often men, like Louis Armstrong and Jelly-Roll Morton. Blues remained a continuing influence on jazz and later on the Beatles and the Rolling Stones.

Somewhat more disputably, I gather, they are said to be the offshoot of the work and sorrow songs of pre-Civil War blacks, improvised in saloons and on street corners, about conflicts with the law, disappointments in love, and the oppression of employers and landlords. To quote one authority, "the blues reflect the cry of the forgotten man and woman, the shout for freedom, the wrath of the frustrated, the ironic chuckle of the fatalist—but also the poverty and hunger of the workless. . . . But let there be no mistake, the blues are also a social music. Today they are of permanent importance as entertainment—ideal music to drink and dance to . . . and, at the other extreme, the song of a segregated class."[8]

Now to try to bring those two together, Kipling and the blues. The simplest way to begin my argument is to point to the group of his poems like "Recessional" and "White Man's Burden." Take stanza one of "Recessional" (1897):

God of our fathers, known of old,
Lord of our far-flung battle-line,
Beneath whose awful Hand we hold
Dominion over palm and pine—
Lord God of Hosts, be with us yet,
Lest we forget—lest we forget![9]

We see there how the declamatory mode is forced on the reader, and how the plangent rhythms (and the Biblical allusions) take the place of music. We note the refrain, and the repetition of the refrain even within the line—so characteristic of blues. We note the confident mixture of pride and melancholy. (For another example, take stanza three—"Far-called, our navies melt away.") Or take stanza one of "White Man's Burden" (1899), though four and seven would be just as good.

Take up the White Man's burden—
Send forth the best ye breed—

> Go bind your sons to exile
> To serve your captives' need;
> To wait in heavy harness,
> On fluttered folk and wild—
> Your new-caught, sullen peoples,
> Half-devil and half-child.[10]

The key idea there—"*our* burden"—is of course the fundamental idea of all blues. "We must serve, bear the burden, and expect no reward." We—that is, those of you assembled here to hear me; while they—the people over there—are the burden.

These are, of course, state poems, addressed one to England, the other to America. They belong to a genre, public and official verse, which is as opposite as is imaginable from the blues. But note that both genres depart, though in opposite directions, equally far from the ordinary bulk of poetry, written about nature or love, and even that written on political themes—think of T. S. Eliot, Robert Frost, Thomas Hardy, Ezra Pound, among Kipling's contemporaries.

Kipling wrote another kind of verse which is superficially much closer to the blues: his Cockney dialect music-hall songs, like "The Widow of Windsor," "Gunga Din," "Fuzzy Wuzzy," and "The Road to Mandalay." In these the language is demotic; the speaker speaks for an oppressed class; the poems were written with tunes— were often sung—and so were much more like blues. The only reason I did not put these first is that they are in some sense fake blues—an impersonation of the oppressed class spokesman—and so less interesting than the first group which are authentically master-class blues. But let us look briefly at one or two of these.

In "The Widow of Windsor" the soldiers of Queen Victoria expressed their pride in serving her. Let us take the first part of stanza two:

> Walk wide o' the Widow at Windsor,
> For 'alf o' Creation she owns:
> We 'ave bought 'er the same with the sword
>   an' the flame,
> An' we've salted it down with our bones.[11]

Of course Kipling is putting words into the mouth of someone at the opposite end of the social scale from himself (and from his primary audience) and those words are what a master-class audience wants to hear; but it's also true that Kipling was a successful writer for the music hall, which was working-class entertainment, and there is no reason to suppose that his work there struck different chords than that of the other writers—for instance, Chaplin's father.

I have said that it was not accidental that Kipling turned to the music hall in just the same years as the blues began to attract attention. This happened because he was rebelling against the system of literature, and the system of taste in his time, as much as they were. For instance, the empire, and even more, imperialist emotions, had been a disgraceful topic, all through British history. It was only Kipling who tried to make it respectable with men of letters in the 1890s. (And though I don't want to get involved in a straight moral defense of Kipling, you must remember that the empire was a fact—a very large fact—and for men of letters not to acknowledge it merely meant that it went on without any moral-imaginative supervision.) The blues and the music hall became an object of elite interest at this time as part of a general revolution in taste by which the cardinal genres of the Victorian consensus, the great novels and essays filled with moral realism and humanism, were being rejected or displaced in favor of more demotic and fragmentary forms. These were the years when circus and carnival, ballet and pantomime, above all perhaps the Commedia dell'Arte, were the really vital kinds of art, while the long novel, in the hands of Galsworthy and Wells, became the province of the philistine. You can see this sensibility formulated in T.S. Eliot's early poetry, and for that matter in the criticism of *The Sacred Wood*. The taste of that time was in some ways for the decadent and over-refined, but in other ways for strong and even coarse effects. That is why the blues and the music hall were the object of elite interest, especially in England and France, where the blues singers were popular much earlier than over here.

Finally, among these Cockney ballads, let us consider "The Road to Mandalay," perhaps the central erotic anecdote of imperialism, the tender romance between a white man and a native beauty, much better than anything he can achieve with an Englishwoman but doomed to end with his desertion of the woman. This is the story of "Madame Butterfly," and Kipling told it several times in fiction in "Without Benefit of Clergy" and "Georgie Porgie." There is a quite triumphalist nostalgia to the melody of the poem. If you know the tune to which it is set, it may remind you of Brecht and Weill in *Mahagonny* or *Threepenny Opera*, which is only just, for Brecht is Kipling's most direct heir. The next to last stanza is classic blues, evoking all the empire around the soldier.

Let me turn now to the second half of my slogan, and say something about the Master Class. I use this term in order to bring out the contrast between Kipling's primary audience and the blues' primary audience, who were an enslaved or at least oppressed class. But I could use other terms, only not "upper class," which I think misses the point. I could call it the ruling class; I shall call it, later, the aristo-military caste; and I could call it, as Orwell does, the official class. Orwell has written a very good essay on Kipling in which he says that Kipling *was* a jingo imperialist, *was* morally insensitive and aesthetically disgusting, but "because he identifies himself with the official class, he does possess one thing which enlightened people seldom or never possess, and that is a sense of responsibility. . . . The official class is always faced with the question, 'In such and such circumstances, what would you *do*?' whereas the opposition is not obliged to take responsibility or make any real decisions."[12] Orwell is there politically attacking the kind of taste which resists Kipling; I am doing the same thing aesthetically.

To give a more specific account of the social types I have in mind when I say Master Class, I can mention a few typical Kipling short stories—for when I speak of his work as blues I mean to cover fiction too. Let me take to begin with the administrators of India—the members of the administrative class of the Indian Civil Service. These were the men whom Kipling joined at the age of seventeen when, returning to India and earning his living as a journalist, he found much of his social life at "the Club." As he said in a later speech, a man's first commission is of great importance, and his placed him among expert masters of men. Nearly all his early work bore on them from some angle or other. *Plain Tales from the Hills* is a collection of stories about their life together at Simla, and other hill-stations, during the hot weather. "Head of District" is a successful and moving story about such an administrator, called Orde, at work in the North of India, who has caught fever in the hills and is carried home but cannot cross the last river home because it is in flood. His wife intrepidly sails across the river to him but arrives too late. As is often the case with Kipling, the pathos of this domestic tragedy is less developed and interesting than the pathos of Orde's relations with his subordinate,

Tallantire, and above all his relations with the men who carry him. They belong to a tribe whom he has personally civilized, in the sense that he has imposed certain civil contracts upon them. They love him as a father; he loves them as his children, fierce fighting men though they be. He gives one his ring, another his watch, as he dies. He has saved nothing, and Tallantire has to promise to collect from friends enough money to send his wife home to England.

The pathos of that will be apparent. The pride comes out, quite savagely, in the other half of the story. After his death, the tribe he has tamed "listens to its priests" (always agents of sedition in Kipling's India) and the British government sends a Bengali to replace Orde. He is a bureaucrat, a babu, and no match for the fighting tribesmen of the north. Trouble breaks out and the tribesmen catch and behead the Bengali's brother. This is enough to scare him off, and at the story's end we understand that the district will be handed back to an Englishman of the master class. The two halves of the story fuse to create another image of the White Man's Burden.

A slightly different social type is the engineer, presented in one of Kipling's finest stories, "The Bridgebuilders." Findlayson has nearly finished building a bridge across the Ganges when the river floods, and his work is in danger of being swept away. Having taken opium to get him through the crisis, Findlayson sees in a vision the river appealing to the gods of India to destroy the work of the English. The gods debate whether the English religion, which is not Christianity but technology—the building of bridges—really is anything new, or whether they can assimilate it as they have in the past assimilated so many other religions. The blues effect is in the dialectical movement to and fro between pride in the bridge and nihilism about any kind of permanence or meaning.

Another type is the army officer, another the doctor, but I'll confine myself simply to the headmaster. He is the figure of ultimate authority in *Stalky and Co.*, Kipling's school book. The boys rebel against, trick, and humiliate the other, inferior figures of authority, the masters, while the Head remains aloof, a semi-divine figure who intervenes only to re-establish justice. But in the climactic story they are able to rebel even against him. He has heroically, but of course secretly, saved a boy's life. Stalky and Co. make this public by cheering him, thus disobeying the rules and getting punished for doing so. Only via disobedience and punishment can the deep and tender love between him and them find expression. That inarticulacy is the blues effect in that case.

Then, as in the case of the poems, there is a notable class of stories which present the same themes, embodied in lower class characters, and with corresponding language, and much more farcical and brutal action. This is true of, for instance, *Soldiers Three*, the volume of stories about soldiers in India. And two very fine stories of this kind are "The Man Who Would Be King" and "Drums of the Fore and Aft."

And in what sense do I apply the term "Blues" to such a variety of Kipling's work? First of all, I do not apply the term to a lot of the Kipling *opus*. I don't for instance to the English history stories, in *Puck of Pook's Hill* and *Rewards and Fairies*, probably Kipling's best work artistically; or to the related country stories, like "The Friendly Brook" or "The Wish House," with pagan and fertility cult values; or to *Kim* or *The Jungle Book* or *Stalky and Co.* —Kipling for children. Of course a strong thematic unity runs through all of Kipling's work. But those I am interested in focus particularly on the master-class man and his *pathos*. (I emphasize the word to stress the German sense, which is broader than the English.) It is thus a thematic reason I am advancing for calling them blues. But there is a formal reason also, and that is their fragmentary and anecdotal and theatrical character. Each is a little fragment of typical experience, cunningly staged and lit by the narrative technique, which has the character not so much of having happened as of having been told and retold. "The Man Who Would Be King" is a good example. These are the anecdotes of British India, or of those clubs of the Empire where the captains and managers and magistrates met. They unite that audience, and formally are like the turns on the vaudeville stage—e.g., "The Green Eye of the Little Yellow God," a melodramatic monologue about the East, rendered by vaudeville performers quite seriously in Kipling's time, and much mocked in subsequent generations. Though artistically and sexually sophisticated, they do not offer a righteous critical account of the experience they describe and so seem naive to critics—because they are out of harmony with criticism.

From the point of view of the history of literature as a whole, I think, it makes most sense to say that Kipling was in love with the aristo-military caste. I call it that to draw attention to the link between the officer class and the aristocracy in every society, no matter how hidden that is in democracies. Much of Kipling's work was an attempt to persuade England to adopt that caste as its leading profile, its self-characterizing representative, instead of the mercantile caste which had before seemed peculiarly English.

And what difference does it make to blues when they are written around and for a master class? This is a difficult question to answer because we must also deal with the shift from music and singer to literature and silent reading. So the answer must be purely speculation and suggestion. Clearly what there is to be blue about changes, from being bossed to being boss. And the part played by the accompaniment, and the improvisation, in the blues is replaced by narrative trick and verbal allusion in the stories.

And what remains the same? First of all the fragmentation of the form, and the oppositeness to, say, *Middlemarch*. There is, in Kipling and in the blues, no reassuring view of society finally handing out roughly fair rewards and punishments, such as was implied by the long majestic narrative of the nineteenth century, however sad the ending. Nor on the other hand is there what you get in twentieth-century Modernist fiction: either the electrically contorted images of indignation of *Catch-22* or *One Flew Over the Cuckoo's Nest*, or the stony wasteland of Beckett of Kafka. It is not Modernist because it is not spiritually rebellious. Above all, both genres serve group solidarity. They make certain people feel good about belonging to the group they belong to, at the cost of rejecting other groups. Any larger social ideas or transcendental ideas of Justice or Truth or the Ideal are shrugged off or comfortably mocked.

But if the two have so much in common, what accounts for the immense difference in the receptivity especially of elite English and American audiences in the 1920s and 1930s, so open to the blues, so closed to Kipling? "During five literary generations," Orwell said in 1942, "every enlightened person has despised Kipling," though he goes on to say, "at the end of that time, nine-tenths of those enlightened persons are forgotten, and Kipling is in some sense still there." The reason, Orwell says, is that "he identified with the ruling power and not with the opposition. In a gifted writer this seems to us strange and even disgusting."[13] That is, we must conclude, a law of our literary imagination.

This was a world-wide phenomenon; you may remember the

important part played by "Some of These Days" in Sartre's *Nausea*;
it reconciles the hero to art, and therefore to life. But Kipling could
never play that part in a novel by Sartre or anyone like him. On the
other hand, one major American writer of the century, Ernest
Hemingway, both declared and demonstrated a considerable debt to
Kipling. But I think that very few of Hemingway's present admirers
notice or respond to that heritage and affiliation of his because they
don't know Kipling and because they overlook that side of Hemingway.

In England, Kipling simply disappeared, without anyone needing
to account for the fact. In 1919 T. S. Eliot reviewed a new volume of
his verse, saying that no one any longer had even a negative opinion of
Kipling—no one even read him. And yet it seems to me clear, now,
that in fact Kipling was a major influence on English writers in the
1920s and 1930s. I mean principally the writers of ironic adventure
tales, from Somerset Maugham to Evelyn Waugh and Graham
Greene. But I think the influence goes much wider than that. I have
been much struck by the prevalence of the habit of covert quotation
and allusion in all sorts of writers after 1918, from P. G. Wodehouse
to Virginia Woolf. In a way that seems to me new, and important
(because it pervades their whole work), they work with pre-formed
types of people, settings, events, and phrases. Nothing is seen freshly
and as for the first time; everything is seen as for the umpteenth time as
manipulable material for ingenious narrative effects. That they surely
learned from Kipling, who is the great master of allusion, rem-
iniscence, and mosaic.

But they denied their father as artist as well as ideologist. For it has
been an unwritten law of our culture that art can offer group identity
and group consolation only to the oppressed; that group consolation
and group identity for the master class is betrayal of art; and that
therefore Kipling is not a significant artist. That is the point—that we
don't feel this as a moral inhibition, though that is what it presumably
is; we feel it as an aesthetic inhibition. But of course once we recognize
that inhibition, we begin to struggle against it and recognize Kipling as
precisely a man of the arts—as almost uniquely so in his close
connections with contemporary music and painting.

So finally I want to describe a link between the different arts at the
turn of the century which is curiously specific to Kipling and to
Boston. This link is made of terracotta; a substance about which I
daresay many readers know more than I—and I should at this point

say that what follows really reports a joint research by me and my Fine Arts Department colleague, Margaret Floyd.

For those who don't know about terracotta, I should say that it belongs in a group of fictile building materials (also including moulded and ornamental brick, tile, mosaic, majolica, and parquetting) which became fashionable in England in the mid-1860s and made possible a new style of architectural ornament particularly appropriate to public buildings. One of its very early uses was on the South Kensington Museums, now called the Victoria and Albert, which were completed in 1869 and were long considered exemplary for architectural terracotta. The link to Boston will become clear when I say that in 1870 the Chairman of the Building Committee for the Boston Museum of Fine Arts wrote to John Sturgis, the Boston architect living in England, saying that they wanted a South Kensington museum here, which Sturgis in fact designed, and it was built, though taken down again in 1906.

This was a significant step in the history of public architecture which Boston took on behalf of the whole United States. The great American museums of the late nineteenth century should be distinguished from earlier ones, Margaret Floyd tells us, because they—those in New York and Philadelphia as well as this one—were the direct outcome of the arts-and-industry movement of England at mid-century. This movement was deeply committed to terracotta, in body, spirit, and purse, to quote another of Margaret's phrases. And since it required a specialized technique of application, and America had no labor force for such work, the Boston Museum terracotta had to be done in England, at the works of J. M. Blashfield, in Stamford, Lincolnshire, and brought over.[14]

The ornamental philosophy of the Victoria and Albert was Renaissance-based, but with a strong oriental influence. A collection of Indian fabrics was a central focus of instruction there, and Owen Jones published his influential volume, *The Alhambra*, in 1841. Another of the key ideas of this movement was the importance of commercial practicability and utility. And terracotta was both very cheap and very flexible—able to imitate exotic materials and artistic effects, and so able to evoke and combine a variety of styles and periods.

John Sturgis began researching museum models for Boston in 1870, when the main façade of the Victoria and Albert at the north of the courtyard had just been completed, in dark red brick, with terracotta ornament in swags, garlands, and sculpture. There was also an arcade of belted and adorned columns in terracotta, and a series of figured mosaic panels and lunettes, illustrating the Arts and Industry. This is typical of all the later uses of the material.

Now the link specific to Kipling comes in the fact that although the designs for this were made by Godfrey Sykes, the actual execution was by John Kipling, who later called himself Lockwood Kipling, the father of Rudyard. His face is one of seven makers of the museum that appear on a frieze there, even though he was then, outside that very narrow and newly-formed world, totally obscure. Though a Wesleyan minister's son, he had turned to the industrial arts in his teens and apprenticed himself to a Burslem potter. There, in 1860, the year he met his wife, he worked on the Wedgwood Institute, a very early example of terracotta ornamentation, done partly by Blashfield. Kipling was too poor to marry until, in 1865, he got a job in India; he went out to teach in a College of Industrial Art in Bombay. The industrial arts movement was spreading out from South Kensington to the empire—and, at the same time, to America. Kipling was sent out to teach terracotta moulding, pottery, and sculpture. And that is where Rudyard Kipling was born in December, 1865.

These links are specific in their touching directly on Boston and Kipling but also in that terracotta was something consciously new, palpably having a career in the world of architecture and social history. But it is possible to make the links more general and show what other things in Kipling's literary work, and Boston's taste for it, can be symbolized by terracotta.

First of all I should say that Lockwood Kipling's career, built on that of terracotta, lifted him to considerable heights of public life, to dining with the Viceroy of India and designing the Durbar Room in the Queen's house at Osborne. He also designed the banners for the ceremony at which she was proclaimed Empress of India in 1877, and he was in charge of the Indian exhibit at the Paris Exposition in 1878. Lockwood Kipling was one of the key makers of the insignia of official splendor at the end of the nineteenth century. And Rudyard, as well as Lockwood, was shaped by this.

Though Rudyard grew up in England, apart from his parents, he spent holidays with his uncle and aunt Burne-Jones and passed a good many days in the South Kensington museums. He was a boy of keen aesthetic interests and tastes, in the Burne-Jones/Morris/Ruskin line. When he rejoined his parents, in Lahore, at seventeen, he found his father head of the Mayo School of Industrial Art there. He himself became a journalist, but this indicated no separation of interest between himself and his parents. Indeed, both of them collaborated, to some hard-to-define degree, on Rudyard's early stories. And most strikingly, his father later illustrated those stories and Kipling's other work. He illustrated them with moulded fictile figures, lit from one side, and photographed with sharp line of shadow. That is to say, the scenes and figures from the son's stories are represented by the father by combining new technologies of reproduction with ancient traditions of dress and posture. That combination is, of course, similar to Rudyard's artistic techniques and shows the essential continuity between the styles of father and son.

Moreover, these illustrations will let us approach the larger significance of terracotta for Kipling's work. They are, for instance, very like the panels and lunettes mentioned before on the Victoria and Albert. All such representations blend the marmoreal and monumental with the anecdotal and journalistic. For instance, you may remember the Lockwood Kipling illustration at the beginning of *Kim*, of the hero sitting on the great gun, Zam-Zamma; he is a shrimp of a lad, about to slip off, and yet at the same time he is marmoreally permanent and immemorially Indian.

This mixed effect seems to me peculiarly appropriate to public buildings which commemorate the passing of time and the succession of new life-forms, new technologies, new machines. And I would like to suggest that the same is true of Kipling's prose, not only in its subjects but in itself, because it combines elements from the Bible and from Shakespeare, from the anthology poets, with elements from the trades, from sports, from military and administrative jargon and up-to-date slang. Many kinds of language and emotional tone are evoked and combined in a kaleidoscope or mosaic, but the two dominant tones are irony about all established values, on the one hand, and a resolute endorsement of those values, on the other. There is something consciously conventional about Kipling's formulations of values, but in the long run they are endorsed or rather enforced—they have gained in power from the irony they have faced and outfaced. In the panels of public buildings the irony is usually slighter but the basic dialectic is the same.

And besides this contrast—organized in terms of nay-saying and yea-saying to authority—there is another range of contrasts in color and texture. In the ornament of the Victoria and Albert, for instance, the tiles and mosaics are often found in brilliantly colored patterns, one pattern juxtaposed to another. Moreover, these colors and textures represent various cultural traditions—a pattern from Persia next to one from Japan, and so on; and from different periods of history—a piece of medieval sculpture next to a piece of Greek. The idea behind the Victoria and Albert sensibility has parameters of history and geography and ultimately of the great adventure of imperialism. I think it would be easy to show that all this is to be found in Kipling's language too and was what Boston responded to.

And above all—to my sense—it is the element of the factitious and meretricious which we find in both Kipling and in the terracotta ornament of public buildings which is most interesting in associating them. By saying factitious I don't mean simply to condemn. I think that at his best Kipling manages to include such elements and transform them artistically; and anyway, the challenge comes ultimately from history—it was the facts of contemporary life which presented artists with unassimilable material to incorporate into art. But there is no denying, especially when we compare this sort of art with that which became its rival and defeated it for a couple of generations—the art of T. S. Eliot in poetry or Picasso in painting—that Kipling's sort has a humiliated air of having sold out to the ruling class. The art of the Armoury Show had a spiritual vitality of rebellion which this Boston art lacked. The Kipling episode was a very brief one, in fact, but it was not shameful. I think we are now in a position to judge it more charitably than we have done during the last seventy-five years; and if we do, I think we shall find a great deal in it of the greatest interest.

NOTES

1. Roger Lancelyn Green, *Kipling: The Critical Heritage* (New York: Barnes and Noble, 1971), p. 68.

2. Green, p. 69.

3. Green, p. 187.

4. Green, p. 173.

5. Green, p. 193.

6. Green, p. 195.

7. Robert Lowell, *Life-Studies* (New York: Noonday Press, 1956, 1959), p. 16.

8. Derrick Stewart-Baxter, *Ma Rainey and the Classic Blues Singers* (New York: Stein and Day, 1970), p. 8.

9. Rudyard Kipling, *A Kipling Pageant* (New York: Literary Guild, 1935), p. 892.

10. Kipling, p. 890.

11. Kipling, p. 912.

12. George Orwell, *Rudyard Kipling: A Collection of Essays* (New York: Doubleday, 1954), p. 126.

13. Orwell, pp. 123, 138.

14. Margaret Henderson Floyd, "A Terra-Cotta Cornerstone for Copley Square: Museum of Fine Arts, Boston, 1870–1876, by Sturgis and Brigham," *Journal of the Society of Architectural Historians,* 32 (March, 1973), 83–103.

Robert Frost:
Society and Solitude

Samuel French Morse

In the antediluvian age of Robert Frost scholarship and studies, Lawrance Thompson observed, "Much has been written on the kinship between [Robert Frost] and Thoreau and Emerson; but not enough. The task which remains is to separate likenesses and differences."[1] By 1973, however, Elaine Barry thought that "enough [had] been written about Frost's philosophical relation to Emerson, and the difference in their attitudes toward the physical world."[2] She did not comment on likenesses; but this omission was corrected, at least in part and with real distinction, by Richard Poirier in *Robert Frost: The Work of Knowing*. Since then the flood of commentary seems to have abated; and at the risk of belaboring the obvious, it is clear that there is something still to be said about the surprising uses to which Frost put the perceptions, biases, and convictions he shared with the Sage of Concord and his most remarkable student. By and large, the insights and attitudes linking him most closely with his Concord mentors were not, as he implied a scholar's or critic's would have been, an "acquirement . . . on assignment, or even self-assignment."[3] Although some of the ideas he undoubtedly encountered for the first time in Emerson's *Poems* and *Essays* did "stick to [him] like burrs" (p.viii), much that seems most Emersonian or Thoreauvian in the poems had its real source in what used to be called similarities of temperament.

We have Frost's own words uttered, as he put it, many years "after sentence,"[4] about some of these perceptions; and we have some demurrers. He objected strongly to what he called Emerson's " 'lack of perception of evil and sin' ";[5] and on at least one occasion he said, " 'I'm not a Thoreauvian; I write about the country but I like the city. I knew very well I wouldn't sell my poetry in the country!' "[6] Nevertheless, an attentive reader can hardly avoid making some connections of his own.

At the beginning of *Nature*, Emerson says that "if a man would be alone," he should "look at the stars."[7] On that particular theme Frost's "star" poems—from the earliest in *A Boy's Will* to "The Milky Way Is a Cowpath" and "One More Brevity" in his last book—provide a complex sequence of variations. Some of the "night pieces," on the other hand—"Desert Places," for example, and "Acquainted with the Night"—reflect an extreme anti-Transcendental view of the solitude in which Emerson found a sublime complement to the society he also cherished. For Frost, solitude often sank into the grief of loneliness and isolation, and that inner emptiness which could "scare" him worse than the "spaces/ Between stars" that terrified Pascal. In this respect, the darker poems add weight to his boast that he was " 'not submissive enough to want to be a follower,' " in spite of his admission that " 'phrases of [Emerson's] began to come to [him] early,' " and that " '[some] of [his] first thinking about [his] own language was certainly Emersonian.' "[8] (It is worth noting here, if only parenthetically, that these somber "night pieces" agree with a famed "orphic utterance"—"Nature always wears the colors of the spirit" [p. 7].)

One has a strong sense that even where Frost's temperament diverged wildly from Emerson's, he may also have learned something about language and metrics that not only "stuck" but served him well in such a melancholy sequence as "The Hill Wife" or in a poem as appallingly bleak as "Bereft":

> Where had I heard this wind before
> Change like this to a deeper roar?
> What would it take my standing there for,
> Holding open a restive door,
> Looking downhill to a frothy shore?
> Summer was past and day was past.
> Somber clouds in the west were massed.
> Out in the porch's sagging floor,
> Leaves got up in a coil and hissed,
> Blindly struck at my knee and missed.

> Something sinister in the tone
> Told me my secret must be known:
> Word I was in the house alone
> Somehow must have gotten abroad,
> Word I was in my life alone,
> Word I had no one left but God (p. 317).

Emerson might have recognized and envied the mastery of accent and the particularity of detail in "Bereft," but its "fable" would almost certainly have appeared to him to have been left unresolved. Nor would he have found in the oblique allusion to the predicament of Job the affirmative "metre-making argument" he looked for in a poem. On the other hand, if Emerson's "Monadnock" really did come " 'pretty near making [Frost] an anti-vocabularian,' "[9] its failure to do so was our good fortune. It seems more plausible to think that Emerson's defective ear and imperfect sense of rhythm bolstered Frost's determination to find in what he liked to call poetry "written regular" all the opportunities he required for the expression of meaning, or, as he said elsewhere, the justification for "any length of line up to six feet,"[10] take that length as you will.

Many of the perceptions and attitudes which for twentieth-century scholars and critics identify Emerson's thought in *Nature* must also have looked like commonplaces to Frost in 1890, and for that very reason open to question and disagreement. Frost said that for his mother's generation "the smart thing when she was young was to be reading Emerson and Poe," just as, he added, it was smart in 1958 "to be reading St. John Perse or T.S. Eliot."[11] Certainly many of the ideas freshly set forth in *Nature* had been repeated and embroidered upon by latter-day admirers and Emersonians, and what had aroused its readers fifty-odd years earlier might well have seemed no more than a confirmation of his own thought by the beginning poet. Moreover, he had other youthful enthusiasms, including Marvell and Rossetti, as Poirier has shown, in addition to Longfellow and, by 1893, Yeats, to quicken his ambition.

Nevertheless, *Nature* gave him much to think about. On the same page with the assertion about looking at the stars one finds another familiar passage, first adapted to his own uses by Thoreau in an even more famous paragraph in *Walden*. Emerson says:

> The charming landscape which I saw this morning is indubitably made up of some twenty or thirty farms. Miller owns this field,

Locke that, and Manning the woodland beyond. There is a
property in the horizon which no man has but he whose eye can
integrate all the parts, that is, the poet. This is the best part of
these men's farms, yet to this their warranty deeds give no title
(pp. 5–6).

This gentle calling into question of the extent and pretensions of
ownership evoked a characteristic response from Thoreau in "Where
I Lived, and What I Lived For." Confident to the point of cockiness in
his account of all but getting "[his] fingers burned by actual
possession" of "the old Hollowell place," Thoreau concludes with
bravado that when the transaction fell through, he "sold" the owner
his farm, as he says, "for just what I gave for it," and "found thus that I
had been a rich man without any damage to my poverty. But I retained
the landscape, and I have since annually carried off what it yielded
without a wheelbarrow."[12] And in a peroration "with respect to
landscapes," he says,

> I have frequently seen a poet withdraw, having enjoyed the most
> valuable part of a farm, while the crusty farmer supposed that he
> had got a few wild apples only. Why, the owner does not know it
> for many years when a poet has put his farm in rhyme, the most
> admirable kind of invisible fence, has fairly impounded it, milked
> it, skimmed it, and got all the cream, and left the farmer only the
> skimmed milk (pp. 106–07).

Neither passage, one may be sure, was wasted on Frost, whose passion
for metaphor occasionally led him to indulge himself in the creation of
figures as complex and tonally ambiguous in their own way as any in
Wallace Stevens, and perhaps even more confusingly so to ideo-
logically oriented critics. Like other "ferocious egoists," Frost valued
his reputation as an "original." It is not, therefore, surprising that
none of his several accounts of the origin and composition of
"Stopping by Woods on a Snowy Evening" mentions Emerson or
Thoreau. On the other hand, the almost boyish delight in the implied
"trespass" recorded in the first stanza—

> Whose woods these are I think I know.
> His house is in the village though;
> He will not see me stopping here
> To watch his woods fill up with snow (p. 275)—

not only echoes the content of both passages but demonstrates almost literally the aptness of Thoreau's notion of the way property can be "put . . . in rhyme" and "impounded." Just how much Frost's conviction that poetry "is metaphor, saying one thing and meaning another, saying one thing in terms of another, the pleasure of ulteriority,"[13] owed to Emerson and Thoreau must remain a matter of some uncertainty; but his fondness for claiming that poetry, like science and philosophy, is "simply made of metaphor"[14] is not very far from the "Introduction" to *Nature* or the final paragraph of *Walden*.

"Stopping by Woods on a Snowy Evening" only begins with a figurative comment on the limits of ownership. It goes on to underscore the isolation of the "I" and the fateful attraction of the woods, "lovely, dark and deep," where solitude blurs into "the darkest evening of the year" and tempts him momentarily from his ordinary commitments to life and, indeed, his commitments to ordinary life, suggested by one of Frost's best-known and most deceptively straightforward metaphors. Whatever one makes of the "promises to keep" and the "miles to go" of the final stanza, they bear out Frost's assertion that he was a "symbolist" of Emersonian stripe, who found it easy to agree with much of the doctrine of language proposed in *Nature*, including the poet's privilege of "mak[ing] free with the most imposing forms and phenomena of the world" (p. 30), though not necessarily with the avowed intention of "assert[ing] the predominance of the soul" (p. 30). That the soul was a crucial concern is clear in such poems as "The Trial by Existence" and "The Silken Tent," where its qualities are those of "devotion" and "sureness"; but if for Frost, as for Emerson and Thoreau, "the vantage point" determines the vision, Frost's perspective is "to earthward":

> If tired of trees I seek again mankind,
>> Well I know where to hie me—in the dawn,
>> To a slope where the cattle keep the lawn.
> There amid lolling juniper reclined,
> Myself unseen, I see in white defined
>> Far off the homes of men, and farther still,
>> The graves of men on an opposing hill,
> Living or dead, whichever are to mind.
>
> And if by noon I have too much of these,
>> I have but to turn on my arm, and lo,
>> The sun-burned hillside sets my face aglow,

> My breathing shakes the bluet like a breeze,
> I smell the earth, I smell the bruisèd plant,
> I look into the crater of the ant (p. 24).

Like his "choice of society" (which was the title for an early
version of "The Vantage Point"), his attitude toward property is
seldom so transcendental as the one expressed in "Stopping by
Woods. . . ." His distaste for being "beholden," whether to his
grandfather for a farm or to a fellow poet for help in the furthering of
his career, could make him ungenerous and vain about what he
regarded as his own, though often with a mixture of self-deprecation
and self-gratification. The uneasiness confessed to in "Trespass"
begins with a modification of Thoreau's assertion that he would
"never paint 'No Admittance' on [his] gate":

> No, I had set no prohibiting sign,
> And yes, my land was hardly fenced,

intended, one suspects, to make the following claim all the more
persuasive:

> Nevertheless the land was mine:
> I was being trespassed on and against (p. 503).

What follows seems clearly intended to be to the credit of the "I" as
well as to his advantage:

> Whoever the surly freedom took
> Of such an unaccountable stay
> Busying by my woods and brook
> Gave me a strangely restless day.
>
> He might be opening leaves of stone,
> The picture-book of the trilobite,
> For which the region round was known,
> And in which there was little property right.
>
> 'Twas not the value I stood to lose
> In specimen crab in specimen rock,
> But his ignoring what was whose
> That made me look again at the clock.
>
> Then came his little acknowledgment:
> He asked for a drink at the kitchen door,
> An errand he may have had to invent,
> But it made my property mine once more (p. 503).

Which seems a familiar and characteristically native assertion of the sacredness of private property and a rather begrudging forgiveness of "those who trespass against us."

Such mixed motives and conflicting attitudes are apparent in Emerson's essay on "Prudence" and in his rather ambiguously expressed feelings about the doctrine of Providence. He was enough of a Puritan and Yankee to concern himself in *The Conduct of Life* with an essay on "Wealth," in which he asserts that "economy mixes itself with morals, inasmuch as it is a peremptory point of virtue that a man's independence be secure"; and he takes note of the fact that "poverty demoralizes." In his way, he was as canny about the advantages of a sound materialism as Poor Richard, and he would have enjoyed Frost's saying about "The Hardship of Accounting":

> Never ask of money spent
> Where the spender thinks it went.
> Nobody was ever meant
> To remember or invent
> What he did with every cent (p. 408).

On the other side, Emerson's "Concord Hymn" evoked from Frost unqualified praise: its "lines [surpassed] any other ever written about soldiers."[15] And it was to Emerson that Frost attributed what he thought of as his sympathy "with subversives, rebels, runners out, runners out ahead, eccentrics, and radicals."[16] His own patriotic poems culminated in "The Gift Outright" and follow in Emerson's footsteps, but they go further in linking what he called "spirit" with "the material-human at the risk of the spirit."[17] It may be just here, in fact, that one gets an inkling of the way likenesses and differences between the two become most apparent.

For Emerson, as Frost liked to point out in what he also called "the greatest Western poem yet," "Unit and universe are round." Frost says, in "On Emerson":

> Another poem could be made from that, to the effect that ideally
> in thought only is a circle round. In practice, in nature, the circle
> becomes an oval. As a circle it has one center—Good. As an
> oval it has two centers—Good and Evil. Thence Monism versus
> Dualism.[18]

Frost's modification of Emerson's circle would seem to have the advantage of agreeing with the "facts" as we know them; but it should not be forgotten that he was also of the opinion that "the fact is the sweetest dream that labor knows" (p. 25), a view which puts him closer to Emerson than he knew, in this one instance at least.

To put it another way: despite Emerson's faith in and hope for individualism, the drift of his thought is all toward the universal and the ideal. The "I" becomes "a transparent eyeball; I am nothing; I see all; the currents of the Universal Being circulate through me; I am part or parcel of God" (p. 6). The drift of Frost's thought is all toward the particular and the actual, toward the self—and in his enlargement of the self, in contrast to Emerson's belief that when "all mean egotism vanishes," then the poet speaks, Frost finds his own poetic identity, for better or worse. It is not surprising to know that Frost said of Emerson that he had the least egotistical of styles.

Frost wanted to believe, as Emerson did, that one had a duty to maintain an optimistic view of things in the face of what looked at times like overwhelming evidence to the contrary. In "Our Hold on the Planet," he puts the case for optimism as unambiguously, one may suppose, as he thought it possible to put it:

> We may doubt the just proportion of good to ill.
> There is much in nature against us. But we forget:
> Take nature altogether since time began,
> Including human nature, in peace and war,
> And it must be a little more in favor of man,
> Say a fraction of one percent at the very least,
> Or our number living wouldn't be steadily more,
> Our hold on the planet wouldn't have so increased
>   (p. 469).

More often, affirmation—or simply the act of composition in which he worked out one possible answer to the question of "what to make of a diminished thing"—seemed "a momentary stay against confusion" and if no more than that, still it was no less. Of such minimal optimism, "Happiness Makes Up in Height What It Lacks in Length" is a prime example:

> Oh, stormy stormy world,
> The days you were not swirled
> Around with mist and cloud,
> Or wrapped as in a shroud,

> And the sun's brilliant ball
> Was not in part or all
> Obscured from mortal view—
> Were days so very few
> I can but wonder whence
> I get the lasting sense
> Of so much warmth and light.
> If my mistrust is right
> It may be altogether
> From one day's perfect weather,
> When starting clear at dawn,
> The day swept clearly on
> To finish clear at eve.
> I verily believe
> My fair impression may
> Be all from that one day
> No shadow crossed but ours
> As through its blazing flowers
> We went from house to wood
> For change of solitude (p. 445).

More often still, Frost's affirmation "snatches a thing from some previous order in time and space into a new order with not so much as a ligature clinging to it of the old place where it was organic" (p. viii), as his own words indicate he wanted it to be.

Of the poems of this kind Frost would seem to be a true master. One example here may suggest others. "After Apple-Picking" is, by common consent, one of the great ones; and in an age of explication, we may even be grateful that it remains intransigently unparaphrasable:

> My long two-pointed ladder's sticking through a
>   tree
> Toward heaven still,
> And there's a barrel that I didn't fill
> Beside it, and there may be two or three
> Apples I didn't pick upon some bough.
> But I am done with apple-picking now.
> Essence of winter sleep is on the night,
> The scent of apples: I am drowsing off.
> I cannot rub the strangeness from my sight
> I got from looking through a pane of glass

I skimmed this morning from the drinking trough
And held against the world of hoary grass.
It melted, and I let it fall and break.
But I was well
Upon my way to sleep before it fell,
And I could tell
What form my dreaming was about to take.
Magnified apples appear and disappear,
Stem end and blossom end,
And every fleck of russet showing clear.
My instep arch not only keeps the ache,
It keeps the pressure of a ladder-round.
I feel the ladder sway as the boughs bend.
And I keep hearing from the cellar bin
The rumbling sound
Of load on load of apples coming in.
For I have had too much
Of apple-picking: I am overtired
Of the great harvest I myself desired.
There were ten thousand thousand fruit to touch,
Cherish in hand, lift down, and not let fall.
For all
That struck the earth,
No matter if not bruised or spiked with stubble,
Went surely to the cider-apple heap
As of no worth.
One can see what will trouble
This sleep of mine, whatever sleep it is.
Were he not gone,
The woodchuck could say whether it's like his
Long sleep, as I describe its coming on,
Or just some human sleep (pp. 88–89).

In "Intellect," Emerson says:

> If you gather apples in the sunshine, . . . and then retire within
> doors and shut your eyes and press them with your hand, you
> shall still see apples hanging in the bright light with boughs and
> leaves thereto . . . for five or six hours afterward. There lie the
> impressions on the retentive organ, though you knew it not. So
> lies the whole series of natural images with which your life has
> made you acquainted, in your memory, though you know it not;
> and a thrill of passion flashes light on their dark chamber, and the

active power seizes instantly the fit image, as the word of its
momentary thought (pp. 296–97).

The passage is intended by Emerson as an illustration of the source
upon which what he calls "the constructive intellect" draws to
produce "thoughts, sentences, poems, plans, designs, systems . . . the
generation of the mind, the marriage of thought with nature." The
process by which the apprehension of the image—the "revelation"
and the "thought"—is transformed into the "picture or sensible
object" in "the language of facts" is the process by which the
poet "break[s] through the silence into adequate rhyme" (p. 297). It
is, as a matter of fact, Emerson's description of how the poet works,
and it foreshadows much that Frost has to say in prose and verse
about his art. Whether "After Apple-Picking" is also an illustration of
the way in which Frost could "snatch a thing from some previous
order" may not greatly matter, any more than it matters whether
Frost's fondness for saying that he wanted to be understood
"wrongly" echoes Emerson's conviction that "to be great is to be
misunderstood." It is, at any rate, best to give Frost both of the last
last words. First, "In a Poem":

> The sentencing goes blithely on its way
> And takes the playfully objected rhyme
> As surely as it keeps the stroke and time
> In having its undeviable say (p. 491).

This would seem to be suitably modest and sufficiently Emersonian to
suit the occasion. The second needs no comment, except to say that it
comes from a late poem he had some trouble with: the lines here
include a final stanza ultimately omitted from "Closed for Good"
when it was published in *In the Clearing*.

> Much as I own I owe
> The passers of the past
> Because their to and fro
> Has cut this road to last,
> I owe them more today
> For having gone away.
>
> . . . .
>
> How often is the case
> I thus pay men a debt

For having left a place
And still do not forget
To pay them some sweet share
For having once been there (p. 576).

NOTES

1. *Robert Frost: The Early Years, 1874–1915* (New York: Holt, Rinehart and Winston, 1966), p. 550.

2. *Robert Frost on Writing* (New Brunswick: Rutgers Univ. Press, 1973), p. 51.

3. "The Figure a Poem Makes" in *Complete Poems of Robert Frost, 1949* (New York: Holt and Company, 1949), p. viii. All references to Frost's poems are to this edition and will be cited hereafter in the text.

4. *Selected Prose of Robert Frost,* ed. Hyde Cox and Edward Connery Lathem (New York: Holt, Rinehart and Winston, 1966), p. 24.

5. Statement attributed to G. R. Elliott in Lawrance Thompson, *Robert Frost: The Years of Triumph, 1915–1938* (New York: Holt, Rinehart and Winston, 1970), p. 570.

6. Quoted in Lawrance Thompson and R. H. Winnick, *Robert Frost: The Later Years, 1938–1963* (New York: Holt, Rinehart and Winston, 1976), p. 331.

7. *The Selected Writings,* ed. Brooks Atkinson (New York: Modern Library, 1950), p. 5. All references to Emerson's writings are to this edition and will be cited in the text.

8. *Robert Frost: The Early Years,* p. 499.

9. *Robert Frost: The Early Years,* p. 499.

10. *Selected Prose of Robert Frost,* p. 26.

11. *Robert Frost: The Early Years,* p. 499.

12. *Walden* (New York: Crowell, 1966), pp. 106–07.

13. *Selected Prose of Robert Frost,* p. 24.

14. *Selected Prose of Robert Frost,* p. 24.

15. *Selected Prose of Robert Frost,* p. 118.

16. *Selected Prose of Robert Frost,* p. 117.

17. *Selected Prose of Robert Frost,* p. 118.

18. *Selected Prose of Robert Frost*, p. 118. "The greatest Western poem yet" refers to Emerson's "Uriel."

45 Mercy Street
and Other Vacant Houses

Linda W. Wagner

It would be a gross oversimplification to attempt to define the "New England tradition" in poetry as intellectual, instructive, patriarchal, British, and somewhat imitative. To use that sense of tradition would be to force such nineteenth-century poets as Emily Dickinson, Ralph Waldo Emerson, Henry David Thoreau, and—to stretch the boundaries a bit—Walt Whitman far outside the accepted patterns: too innovative, too American, too emotional, and certainly too personal, these poets were already working toward achieving a distinctly unique poetic voice, a concept we today regard as "modern." To illustrate, what a difference between the well-known lines of a poet who represents the formal New England poetic tradition, William Cullen Bryant, and those of Dickinson, Emerson, Whitman:

> To him who in the love of Nature holds
> Communion with her visible forms, she speaks
> A various language; for his gayer hours
> She has a voice of gladness, and a smile
> And eloquence of beauty, and she glides
> Into his darker musings, with a mild
> And gentle sympathy. . . .
> > "Thanatopsis"

> I celebrate myself, and sing myself,
> And what I assume you shall assume,
> For every atom belonging to me as good belongs
> > to you

> I loafe and invite my soul,
> I lean and loafe at my ease observing a spear
>   of summer grass.
>
> My tongue, every atom of my blood, form'd from
>   this soil, this air,
> Born here of parents born here from parents the
>   same, and their parents the same,
> I, now thirty-seven years old in perfect
>   health begin,
> Hoping to cease not till death.[1]

When Whitman shares with us his biography (and nickname)—the fact that he is 37, a loafer, an American and expansive in his American confidence—we respond to that identity, that reaching out. "Camerado, this is no book," he writes in "So Long"; "Who touches this touches a man. . . . From behind the screen where I hid I advance personally solely to you" (p. 391). A new definition of the poem as a means of speaking intimately evolves here, not only with Whitman but with Emerson in "The Problem":

> I like a church; I like a cowl;
> I love a prophet of the soul;
> And on my heart monastic aisles
> Fall like sweet strains, or pensive smiles;
> Yet for all his faith can see
> Would I that cowled churchman be. . . . [2]

Simultaneously but very separately, in her timid yet strangely assertive voice, Emily Dickinson began the same process of using personal speech in poems that defied both classification and publication:

> I tie my Hat—I crease my Shawl—
> Life's little duties do—precisely. . . . [3]
>
> I am alive—I guess
> The branches on my Hand
> Are full of Morning Glory— (pp. 225–26).
>
> This is my letter to the World
> That never wrote to Me— (p. 211).
>
> I was the slightest in the House—
> I took the smallest Room—
> At night, my little Lamp, and Book—

And one Geranium— (p. 234).

These are hardly poems marked by any tones of imitation, any deference toward the Mother Country and its poetics, or any attempt to set forth large statements of intellectual weight. They are beginnings rather than culminations, forerunners of modern poetry rather than inheritors of an eighteenth-century mode. And they are strangely ungeographical, placed much more directly in the province of the heart than in any New England location. The conflict that must have existed between poetic convention—the use of place, landscape, to reveal larger ideas; the absence of the personal; the use of poetic diction rather than normal speech rhythms—and the interiority of these poems probably accounted for much of the poets' satisfaction with them.

From Dickinson's room in the family home in Amherst, Massachusetts, to Anne Sexton's lost family home on Mercy Street is only a brief walk. The wallpaper may be different, given the century that divides the houses, but the atmosphere is distressingly similar: both Sexton's and Dickinson's poems speak of the need for an identity as a writer and of their search for a male authority figure—father, brother, editor, analyst, husband, minister, critic, fellow writer—to support that writing process. The poems share a tone of apology for their emotional, feminine subject matter (as contrasted with supposedly "intellectual" themes) and an awareness on the part of each poet that this work is innovative, unconventional, and that it exists almost as a flight from accepted traditions. Both Sexton's and Dickinson's poems are marked with exuberance, anger, guilt, frustration, and, finally, self-acceptance. The best account of these dichotomies between a woman's trying to come, aggressively, to art while simultaneously trying to survive in a social context that demands passivity is the recent *Madwoman in the Attic* by Susan Gubar and Sandra M. Gilbert. Their readings of Dickinson's poems explain full well her reclusive, questioning, unsure yet dramatic poetic persona; and the extensions one can make from Dickinson to some of the best-known New England poets of this century are clear.[4]

Without benefit of criticism or sociology, Anne Sexton captures these contradictions in the title poem from *45 Mercy Street*. Published posthumously in 1976, this collection creates a paradigm of the non-traditional poet's journey, the movement from the need for a place in the accepted mainstream to the strength to stand outside. The hegira that begins the book is, tellingly, a female hegira; and Sexton defines the journey as "a means of escaping from an undesirable or dangerous environment" as well as "a means of arriving at a highly desirable destination." Where are the models, in the canon of American literature, for a woman's initiation story? Where are the portraits of the young woman as artist? Here.

With "45 Mercy Street," Sexton creates that story, that portrait. She gives us Mercy and other subtle echoes of the "Twenty-third Psalm" throughout the collection: "Surely goodness and mercy shall/ follow me all the days of my life;/ and I will dwell in the house of the/ Lord for ever." Sexton plays with *surely*, the female expectation of living a good, modest, loving life and being rewarded; with *goodness*, in both a social and sexual sense; and she sets those words against a recurring theme of *mercy*, the particularly female capacity for compassion that is non-judgmental. Inherent in Sexton's portrayal is the female ability to accept, to forgive; not surprisingly, the characters of these last Sexton poems are almost entirely female—her daughters Linda and Joy, her mother, grandmother, great aunt Nana, friends.

> In my dream,
> drilling into the marrow
> of my entire bone,
> my real dream,
> I'm walking up and down Beacon Hill
> searching for a street sign—
> namely MERCY STREET.
> Not there.
>
> I try the Back Bay.
> Not there.
> Not there.
> And yet I know the number.
> 45 Mercy Street.
> I know the stained-glass window
> of the foyer,
> the three flights of the house
> with its parquet floors.
> I know the furniture and
> mother, grandmother, great-grandmother,
> the servants.
> I know the cupboard of Spode,

> the boat of ice, solid silver,
> where the butter sits in neat squares
> like strange giant's teeth
> on the big mahogany table.
> I know it well.[5]

Sexton here accepts both the reality of dream, "real dream," and her
need to find sources, home—and how maternal a home; she is also in
her refrain affirming her own knowledge—"I know," "I know."
Reality hits her with its contradictions, however, for no matter that she
knows this house, knows it with the acute memories of the child, she
cannot find it.

What she does find, in the next two stanzas, are the dichotomies
inherent in being the female child: "When she was good, she was very,
very good":

> Where did you go?
> 45 Mercy Street,
> with great-grandmother
> kneeling in her whale-bone corset
> and praying gently but fiercely
> to the wash basin,
> at five A.M.
> at noon
> dozing in her wiggy rocker,
> grandfather taking a nip in the pantry,
> grandmother pushing the bell for the downstairs
>   maid,
> and Nana rocking Mother with an oversized flower
> on her forehead to cover the curl
> of when she was good and when she was. . . .
> And where she was begat
> and in a generation
> the third she will beget,
> me,
> with the stranger's seed blooming
> into the flower called *Horrid*.

> I walk in a yellow dress
> and a white pocketbook stuffed with cigarettes,
> enough pills, my wallet, my keys,
> and being twenty-eight, or is it forty-five?
> I walk. I walk.
> I hold matches at the street signs

for it is dark,
as dark as the leathery dead
and I have lost my green Ford,
my house in the suburbs. . . .
and I am walking and looking
and this is no dream
just my oily life
where the people are alibis
and the street is unfindable for an
entire lifetime.

The significance of the poem's being titled "45 Mercy Street" instead
of just "Mercy Street," as was her earlier play, now becomes clear.
Sexton is 45. She will die at 45, just a scant month before turning 46.
These chronological markings are as important to Sexton as is her
astrological profile—Scorpios both, she and Plath, marked, she
thought, by violence, unkindness, will.[6] Married at seventeen, Sexton
found herself in her poetry at 28. That age, then, is important to her; it
represents the myth that people *do* find themselves, do mature, do
become independent. Even after her divorce from the man who had
husbanded her since she was 17, Sexton could not find that
independence she seemed to prize so highly, and her anger, her
disillusion, at this recognition leads to the stanza of withdrawal,
denial, and finally a return to her own womanliness as her chief
identity:

Pull the shades down—
I don't care!
Bolt the door, mercy,
erase the number,
rip down my street sign,
what can it matter,
what can it matter to this cheapskate
who wants to own the past. . . .

Not there.

I open my pocketbook,
as women do. . . .

Next I pull the dream off
and slam into the cement wall
of the clumsy calendar
I live in,

>   my life,
>   and its hauled up
>   notebooks.

Sexton as poet (Dickinson as poet, Plath as poet)—can we accept the persona as writer only, unmoored, lost, admittedly searching, unlocateable, certainly NOT New England bound. We can hear Sexton laugh as she writes to Jon Stallworthy in 1967, "I adore being called the Nefertiti of New England."[7] In 1963, to Robert Lowell, she had admitted, "One of these days, I will learn to bear to be myself."[8] The poems of *45 Mercy Street* show that bearing, that becoming, and the anger in having to remain outside an accepted tradition, both geographic and poetic.

Always "confessional," usually "hysterical," always maligned for poems written to menstruation, lovers, abortions, her uterus, Sexton turns to apology for that personal element, as in "Talking to Sheep," or to questioning her multiple roles, as in "The Falling Dolls":

>   Dolls,
>   by the thousands,
>   are falling out of the sky
>   and I look up in fear
>   and wonder who will catch them?

Guilt—why are you a poet? Who's taking care of your children (daughters)?

>   . . . I dream, awake, I dream of falling dolls
>   who need cribs and blankets and pajamas
>   with real feet in them.
>   Why is there no mother?
>   Why are all these dolls falling out of the sky?
>   Was there a father?
>   Or have the planets cut holes in their nets
>   and let our childhood out,
>   or are we the dolls themselves,
>   born but never fed? (pp. 10–11).

As with her earlier collections, some of the best poems in *45 Mercy Street* are Sexton's poems to her children, but here the simple sense of love and responsibility—an awesome responsibility—is coupled with an anguish of lost identity, of lost place: *are we the dolls themselves?*

Parallel with that sense of loss, increasing because of that disorientation, runs a terrible, oppressive responsibility. Even the animal poems are marked with the maternal guilt, as when Sexton laments to a dead animal, "Mole dog,/ I wish your mother would wake you up." The divorce poems carry similar guilt. Whether the wife is re-attaching her husband's severed hands and feet or worrying about her teenage daughters ("we, mothers, crumpled and flyspotted/ with bringing them this far/ can do nothing now but pray"), the female persona bears the responsibility. Not easily. Undeniably. She is born to it. As Sexton writes in "The Big Boots of Pain,"

> I would sell my life to avoid
> the pain that begins in the crib. . . .
> when the planets drill
> your future into you
> for better or worse
> as you marry life
> and the love that gets doled out
> or doesn't (p. 103).

The gamble of the traditional woman's life, be she Cinderella or Sexton, is her marriage, and that marriage is her primary responsibility. That such a single responsibility, carried singly, may wear into madness is the image of the poet's crucifixion in "The Passion of the Mad Rabbit":

> Next it was bad Friday and they nailed me up
> like a scarecrow and many gathered eating pop-
>   corn, carrying
> hymnals or balloons. There were three of us there,
> though *they* appeared normal. My ears, so pink like
>   powder
> were nailed. My paws, sweet as baby mittens, were
>   nailed.
> And my two fuzzy ankles. I said, "Pay no attention.
>   I am crazy."
> And some giggled and some knelt. My oxygen
>   became tiny
> and blood rang over and over in my head like a bell.
> The others died, the luck of it blurting through them.
> I could not. I was a silly broken umbrella
> and oblivion would not kiss me. For three days it
> was thus.

Then they took me down and had a conference.
It is Easter, they said, and you are the Easter
    Bunny.
Then they built a great pyre of kindling and laid me
    on top
and just before the match they handed me a pink
    basket
of eggs the color of the circus.
Fire lit, I tossed the eggs to them, *Hallelujah* I sang
    to the eggs,
singing as I burned to nothing in the tremor of the
    flames.
My blood came to a boil as I looked down the throat
    of madness,
but singing yellow egg, blue egg, pink egg, red egg,
    green egg,
Hallelujah, to each hard-boiled-colored egg . . .
                           (pp. 90–91).

Poor lost Alice in Wonderland; poor mother, responsible for any ritual, tradition, food, spirit; poor woman lost in sexuality, fertility, the flames of lust and madness—here as in *Transformations* Sexton makes use of our common heritage of fairy tale, myth, archetype of sex goddess/mother, and poises it against that other set of opposites, sanity/insanity. She similarly uses the image of angel food in her poem about the virgin/whore identity, wishing to change her name from Anne to Mary (her mother's name); wishing for purity, for grace, and finally—pervasively—for mercy:

I kneel once more,
in case mercy should come . . . (p. 89).

finding my Mercy Street,
kissing it and tenderly gift-wrapping my love . . .
                              (p. 105).

Much as she hopes for mercy, tired and resentful as she is of life's non-acceptance and its demands, still Sexton comes in these last poems to the confidence of her own self-possession. There is contentment of a sort in *45 Mercy Street*. There are images throughout the collection of houses, shelters gained through love, homes. The ultimate image of place occurs in her poem "Keeping the

City." Lost from even that maternal ancestry, searching as she
honestly recounts, Sexton yet finds her strength in her kinship with her
maturing daughters, and through them, with herself as woman. Her
strength is, however, but fragile, tentative, a veil of bright motion, a
daisy, which some eyes might consider ineffectual:

> The city
> of my choice
> that I guard
> like a butterfly, useless, useless
> in her yellow costume, swirling
> swirling around the gates.
> The city shifts, falls, rebuilds . . . (p. 24).

That place, unnamed as it is, that city, is, finally, of Sexton's *choice*—
and her ability to make that choice is crucial. And while it is not a New
England city but a much more interior and specifically female city, it
does, finally, "rebuild."

The same sense of alienation, of being dis- or mis-located,
permeates the poetry of Sylvia Plath as well. The torture of attempting
to create a safe home anguishes her late poems, particularly those of
Ariel and *Crossing the Water*, when the poet/persona, like that of
Sexton, bears the responsibility for not only her own children but the
world's lost souls. As Plath promises in her poem to her son, "Nick
and the Candlestick,"

> Love, love,
> I have hung our cave with roses.
> With soft rugs—
> The last of Victoriana.[9]

In this safe room, Plath can contend bravely,

> Let the stars
> Plummet to their dark address,
>
> Let the mercuric
> Atoms that cripple drip
> Into the terrible well. . . .

She has found her solidity—her children, her sense of self, her work.
As her poem to her friend and nurse, "Kindness," declares,

> Kindness glides about my house.
> Dame Kindness, she is so nice!

> The blue and red jewels of her rings smoke
> In the windows, the mirrors
> Are filling with smiles. . . .
> And here you come, with a cup of tea
> Wreathed in steam.
> The blood jet is poetry,
> There is no stopping it.
> You hand me two children, two roses (p. 82).

These are hardly the typical Plath poems so often anthologized. Plath's more common poems, throughout her career, are those of search. Even as a young poet, she images herself as alienated, different. Displaced at home, displaced at Smith, displaced in New York in the fashionable offices of *Mademoiselle*, she finally seems to have found a sympathetic locale in England. She loved its tranquility, its traditions, during her years at Oxford; and once she and Ted Hughes had decided to live in England rather than America, she wrote her mother,

> I am growing very pleased with the idea of living in England. The speed and expense of America is just about 50 years ahead of me. I could be as fond of London as of any other city in the world, and plays, books, and all these things are so much more within one's means. . . . I want Ted to take me on a trip around England, especially to Wales and to little fishing villages. When you come, we should go on a jaunt of some sort, staying at old inns and taking country walks.[10]

Throughout her late poems, it becomes clear that Plath saw herself as old-fashioned, virtuous, pure. Set against her husband's adultery, his betrayal of what she had found to be a perfect marriage, one that combined satisfaction in work with satisfaction in love, her sense of place and tradition becomes wound into her sense of self and even of morality.

Given Plath's personal situation in 1963, separated from Hughes, living in the house Yeats once inhabited, entirely responsible for the children, Frieda and Nicholas, her feelings of personal bitterness may have colored her view of her country. In her 1963 essay "America! America!" Plath faults her superficial American education for its emphasis on conformity. "Eccentricities, the perils of being *too* special, were reasoned and cooed from us like sucked thumbs."[11]

Because there is no place in America for "the embryo rebel, the artist, the odd," Plath happily relinquishes her identity as American. As she muses in "Three Women,"

> I shall meditate upon normality.
> I shall meditate upon my little son. . . .
> I do not will him to be exceptional.
> It is the exception that interests the devil.
> It is the exception that climbs the sorrowful hill
> Or sits in the desert and hurts his mother's heart.
> I will him to be common,
> To love me as I love him,
> And to marry what he wants and where he will.[12]

The contradictions inherent in saying one is more or less British or more or less American (and Plath's poetry implies that Hughes was certainly more American than she, in a negative sense; just as he was also German, Nazi, Panzer-man) surface again in a 1962 essay titled "Ocean 1212-W." Plath speaks here of her passionate love for the sea,

> My childhood landscape was not land but the end of the land—the cold, salt, running hills of the Atlantic. I sometimes think my vision of the sea is the clearest thing I own. I pick it up, exile that I am, like the purple "lucky stones" I used to collect with a white ring all the way round, or the shell of a blue mussel with its rainbowy angel's fingernail interior; and in one wash of memory the colors deepen and gleam, the early world draws breath.
> Breath, that is the first thing. Something is breathing. My own breath? The breath of my mother? No, something else, something larger, farther, more serious, more weary.[13]

Replacing identity, replacing the mother as source of life and breath, the sea became Plath's alter ego. She refers to herself in this essay as both "an exile" and a "reject"; yet she had found solace and an essential part of her person—"my love of change and wildness"—in these early years by the sea, living in the "sea-bitten house" that was lost with her father's death. Plath mourns "those nine first years of my life sealed themselves off like a ship in a bottle—beautiful, inaccessible, obsolete, a fine, white flying myth."

It is not accidental that, in Plath's beautifully tranquil poem "Morning Song," her hymn to her new-born son, his cry returns her to that beloved seaside:

> All night your moth-breath
> Flickers among the flat pink roses. I wake to listen:
> A far sea moves in my ear.
>
> One cry, and I stumble from bed, cow-heavy
>   and floral
> In my Victorian nightgown.
> Your mouth opens clean as a cat's. The window
>   square
>
> Whitens and swallows its dull stars. And now
>   you try
> Your handful of notes;
> The clear vowels rise like balloons (p. 1).

The poet's yearning for a like tranquility is the theme of Plath's masterful "Tulips." The old man's death in "Berck-Place" is imaged to be like the sea, "a green sea/ . . . fold upon fold far off, concealing hollows." The woman on horseback in "Ariel" reaches her moment of climax in a similar sea image: "And now I/ Foam to wheat, a glitter of seas. . . ."

Plath's recognition of the central importance of primal themes in poetry in some ways explicates this recurrence of the sea image. The 1962 comment to follow is written with that tinge of defiance that shows Plath's defensiveness, and reminds us of the true alienation of Dickinson, Sexton, and Plath from both the world of the traditional poet and similarly, and because of their poetry, from the world of the traditional woman:

> My poems do not turn out to be about Hiroshima, but about a child forming itself finger by finger in the dark. They are not about the terrors of mass extinction, but about the bleakness of the moon over a yew tree in a neighboring graveyard. Not about the testaments of tortured Algerians, but about the night thoughts of a tired surgeon.
>
>   In a sense, these poems are deflections. I do not think they are an escape. For me, the real issues of our time are the issues of every time—the hurt and wonder of loving; making in all its forms—children, loaves of bread, paintings, buildings; and the conservation of life of all people in all places. . . .[14]

Plath's mention of her yew tree poem sends us to one of the most central poems in *Ariel*. Unrelieved anguish is its tone, imaged in the "blackness and silence" of the closing, the "complete despair" of the shut, starkly white moon. What the scene of the yew tree in the graveyard, pointing up through the bluish light toward the moon, does, in effect, is to convince the poet/persona that all her beliefs are in error. She searches for a mother, a spirit of tenderness, and finds nothing—either in the moon, in the Virgin, or in her own mother. Church bells, nature, human relations have all disappointed her. Of herself, the poet tells us only "I have fallen a long way," "How I would like to believe in tenderness," "I simply cannot see where there is to get to."

If vacillation marks many of Plath's late poems, a pulling between affirmation and negation, then "The Moon and the Yew Tree" is striking in its outright denial. It parallels "Medusa," in which Plath asks of her mother's presence, "Did I escape, I wonder?" and "Getting There," the most forbidding of Plath's journey poems, in which life is pictured as a war and the poet/persona described as a struggling refugee "dragging my body/ Quietly through the straw of the boxcars."

> It is Adam's side,
> This earth I rise from, and I in agony.

All the refugee wants is a place, a destination: "It is so small/ The place I am getting to, why are there these obstacles." Yet she despairs repeatedly

> Is there no still place
> Turning and turning in the middle air,
> Untouched and untouchable. . . .

Even in the midst of her anguished search, however, she bears responsibility for the other despairing travelers: "I shall bury the wounded like pupas,/ I shall bury and count the dead." Here again, and throughout Plath's late poems, are the themes of the Sexton poems: the search for place and support, the disassociation from the expected, the assumption of grave responsibilities, and finally the acceptance of both the self and its place—always partial, disappointing, dismaying: "No where." "I do not fear it: I have been there." "Starless and fatherless, a dark water."

One of Plath's most direct poems which deals with the loss of place—and, accordingly, with the loss of the myth that women are to

be cared for, protected, housed, by men—is "Letter in November."
One assumes a final letter from her estranged husband, close to the
time of her thirtieth birthday—Plath like Sexton was a Scorpio and,
more important, believed that she was plagued with the Scorpian
doubleness[15]—for the poem opens addressing him:

> Love, the world
> Suddenly turns, turns colour. The streetlight
> Splits through the rat's-tail
> Pods of the laburnum at nine in the morning.
> It is the Arctic,
>
> This little black
> Circle. . . .

This is the world Plath was born to, one of a man's building, now only
a "little black circle, the Arctic." Instead, as the world suddenly turns,
the poet has found her *own* world; most of the poem gives us her
possession of that world, through a simple life-affirming subject-verb
structure. And, as often in Plath's late poetry, the subject is *I*:

> I am flushed and warm.
> I think I may be enormous,
> I am so stupidly happy,
> My Wellingtons
> Squelching and squelching through the beautiful
>   red.
>
> This is my property.
> Two times a day
> I pace it, sniffing
> The barbarous holly with its viridian
> Scallops, pure iron,
>
> And the wall of old corpses.
> I love them.
> I love them like history.
> The apples are golden,
> Imagine it—
>
> My seventy trees
> Holding their gold-ruddy balls. . . .

The tone changes abruptly, whether with some reference to the
chilling Midas touch, that gold like this is unnatural, or more directly
with reference to the letter of the title: outwardly the persona has won;

she has her place; she has created it. Inwardly, however, the victory of possession—alone—is hollow. The poem closes,

> My seventy trees
> Holding their gold-ruddy balls
> In a thick grey death-soup,
> Their million
> Gold leaves metal and breathless.
>
> O love, O celibate.
> Nobody but me
> Walks the waist-high wet.
> The irreplaceable
> Golds bleed and deepen, the mouths of
> Thermopylae.

The same duality—pride in survival, dismay at abandonment—dominates the marvelous sequence of bee poems, "The Bee Meeting," "The Arrival of the Bee Box," "Stings," "The Swarm," and "Wintering." The identity of the old queen seems to represent Plath—as old wife, old poet, soon to be displaced by Hughes' new lover:

> . . . They are hunting the queen.
> Is she hiding, is she eating honey?
> She is very clever.
> She is old, old, old, she must live another
> year, and she knows it.

Yet for all her endurance and cleverness, the old queen is "exhausted . . . exhausted. . . . The magician's girl who does not flinch." All the knives of pain do not, finally, hurt as much as they might because the poet/persona sees herself as being in control: "I ordered this, this clean wood box." "Bare-handed, I hand the combs."

In the poem "Stings," Plath shifts from identity as queen bee to identity as woman-observer robbed of her uniqueness in the process of domesticity:

> I stand in a column
>
> Of winged, unmiraculous women,
> Honey-drudgers.
> I am no drudge
> Though for years I have eaten dust
> And dried plates with my dense hair.

> And seen my strangeness evaporate,
> Blue dew from dangerous skin.
> Will they hate me,
> These women who only scurry,
> Whose news is the open cherry, the open clover?
>
> It is almost over.
> I am in control.

Fearful that other women will not accept her, the persona yet refuses to deny her power, her strangeness; and at the end of "Stings" the identities fuse so that the final image—of powerful femaleness turned to destruction against male confinement—parallels the ending of "Lady Lazarus." In that poem, the woman persona rises from death by fire:

> Ash, ash—
> You poke and stir.
> Flesh, bone, there is nothing there—
>
> A cake of soap,
> A wedding ring,
> A gold filling.
>
> Herr God, Herr Lucifer,
> Beware
> Beware.
>
> Out of the ash
> I rise with my red hair
> And I eat men like air.

In "Stings," the rebirth depends less on anger against a single male prosecution or betrayal than it does on the woman's self-awareness. Rebirth is as much a personal discovery as it is a vindication:

> They thought death was worth it, but I
> Have a self to recover, a queen.
> Is she dead, is she sleeping?
> Where has she been,
> With her lion-red body, her wings of glass?
>
> Now she is flying
> More terrible than she ever was, red
> Scar in the sky, red comet
> Over the engine that killed her—

The mausoleum, the wax house.

Place as house, wax house, mausoleum, confinement, death: Plath's
images of would-be triumph are almost unbearable, but she softens
the impact of "house" in the last poem of the bee sequence,
"Wintering."

> This is the easy time, there is nothing doing.
> I have whirled the midwife's extractor,
> I have my honey,
> Six jars of it,
> Six cat's eyes in the wine cellar,
>
> Wintering in a dark without window
> At the heart of the house . . . .

Somnolent, peaceful, woman in possession of spoils—rather than
being a possession herself—there is a calm here, an acceptance, first
in the direct statement,

> The bees are all women,
> Maids and the long royal lady.
> They have got rid of the men,
>
> The blunt, clumsy stumblers, the boors.
> Winter is for women—

and finally in the affirmation of the last stanza,

> Will the hive survive, will the gladiolas
> Succeed in banking their fires
> To enter another year?
> What will they taste of, the Christmas roses?
> The bees are flying. They taste the spring.

For all her emphasis on endurance, Plath's poems leave us rather
with the anguish, the sense of displacement, the search for place, the
terrible weight of responsibility. In Plath as in Sexton, in Dickinson as
in Rich, the themes recur, pointing repeatedly to the double disenfran-
chisement, the double disorientation of being both writer and woman.
I had intended to include two other poets, the vibrant and strangely
androgynous E. E. Cummings and the divided but responsive Robert
Lowell. Reminiscent as many of their poems are of the New England
heritage, their poems differ greatly from those of Dickinson, Plath,
and Sexton: the defiance against tradition is more often intellectual-

ized, controllable. The refusal to conform is itself a pose and, in that, more acceptable. As Richard Kennedy points out in his fine biography of Cummings,

> despite his hostility to American culture, he is as American as Concord Bridge and the Statue of Liberty. "The tradition, after all, in this nation is bucking the tradition. . . ."[16]

Acceptance of attitudes, an intellectual understanding of defiance: our male writers feel secure enough in their roles as artists, and the cultural expectations of those roles, that they can deal with alienation and even with loss of place, parents, love. There is much less sense of torture, much less search imagery in the poems of Cummings and Lowell, and more of a tendency to offer wisdom, panacea, achieved knowledge. Just as in "Thanatopsis" Bryant's view of that final search, that final definition of place—death— is highly intellectualized:

> When thoughts
> Of the last bitter hour come like a blight
> Over thy spirit, and sad images
> Of the stern agony, and shroud, and pall,
> And breathless darkness, and the narrow house,
> Make thee to shudder, and grow sick at heart;—
> Go forth under the open sky, and list
> To Nature's teachings. . . .

Death as "pleasant dreams" in the Bryant poem has no echo in the work of Dickinson, Sexton, or Plath. The fact of actual death is the price we have all paid for their great alienation; the loss of place, the hostility of non-acceptance becomes the image throughout the poems so that Sexton may write, in *Words for Dr. Y,*

> Home is my Bethlehem
> my succoring shelter[17]

but just as quickly admit "Houses haunt me. . . ."

> I am alone here in my own mind.
> There is no map
> and there is no road . . . (p. 63).

Lest we be tempted to read the pervasive images of Sexton's and Plath's poems as only contemporary, striking evidence of the interiority of the modern poetic focus, we must return to the poems of Emily Dickinson:

> One need not be a Chamber—to be Haunted—
> One need not be a House—
> The Brain has corridors—surpassing
> Material Place. . . .[18]

Isolation, loss of place, responsibility, guilt, the creation of a new world—alone, alone as both artist and woman. The New England tradition seems far removed from these poets, who are, perhaps, among our greatest. We should reach this recognition, I think, with less anger than with lament, for, as Dickinson wrote in 1863, one hundred years before Plath's suicide:

> Victory comes late—
> And is held low to freezing lips—
> Too rapt with frost
> To take it—
> How sweet it would have tasted—
> Just a drop. . . .
>
> Crumbs—fit such little mouths—[19]

NOTES

1. Walt Whitman, *Leaves of Grass and Selected Prose,* ed. John Kouwenhoven (New York: Modern Library), pp. 23–24. Subsequent references are cited in the text.

2. Ralph Waldo Emerson, "The Problem" in *The Norton Anthology of American Literature,* I, eds. Gottesman, Holland, Kalstone, et al. (New York: W. W. Norton, 1979), p. 833.

3. *The Complete Poems of Emily Dickinson,* ed. Thomas H. Johnson (Boston: Little, Brown and Co., 1960), p. 212. Subsequent references are cited in the text.

4. Sandra M. Gilbert and Susan Gubar, *The Madwoman in the Attic: The Woman Writer and the Nineteenth-Century Literary Imagination* (New Haven: Yale Univ. Press, 1979). That there still exists a sense of the modern "New England" poet seems clear from looking at the Table of Contents in Donald Hall's anthology *Contemporary American Poetry* (New York: Penguin Books, 1972). Nearly 75 percent of the 39 poets included are either from New England or were educated there. Of the 39 poets, only four—Sexton, Plath, Rich, and Denise Levertov—are women; and of those four,

Levertov is British and the other three are all New Englanders.

5. Anne Sexton, *45 Mercy Street,* ed. Linda Gray Sexton (Boston: Houghton Mifflin Co., 1976), p. 3. Hereafter cited in text.

6. Sexton's sequence of poems "Scorpio, Bad Spider, Die: The Horoscope Poems" was published in 1978 in the collection *Words for Dr. Y, Uncollected Poems with Three Stories,* ed. Linda Gray Sexton (Boston: Houghton Mifflin Co.). There are frequent references in both Sexton's and Plath's poetry and letters to astrology.

7. Included in *Anne Sexton, A Self-Portrait in Letters,* ed. Linda Gray Sexton and Lois Ames (Boston: Houghton Mifflin Co., 1977), p. 318.

8. *Anne Sexton,* p. 170.

9. Sylvia Plath, *Ariel* (New York: Harper and Row, 1965), p. 34. Hereafter cited in text.

10. *Letters Home by Sylvia Plath: Correspondence 1950–1963,* ed. Aurelia Schober Plath (New York: Harper and Row, 1975), p. 356.

11. Included in *Johnny Panic and the Bible of Dreams, Short Stories, Prose, and Diary Excerpts* (New York: Harper and Row, 1979), p. 54.

12. Sylvia Plath, "Three Women: A Poem for Three Voices," *Winter Trees* (New York: Harper and Row, 1972), p. 62.

13. *Johnny Panic,* p. 20.

14. *Johnny Panic,* p. 64.

15. Many references to astrology pepper Plath's work, perhaps the most effective being the ending of "Words" (*Ariel,* p. 85): "While/ From the bottom of the pool, fixed stars/ Govern a life."

16. Richard S. Kennedy, *Dreams in the Mirror: A Biography of E. E. Cummings* (New York: Liveright, 1980), p. 7.

17. *Words for Dr. Y.,* p. 61. Hereafter cited in text.

18. *Complete Poems,* p. 333.

19. *Complete Poems,* p. 340.

Recent New England Fiction: Outsiders and Insiders

Melvin J. Friedman

Eternal summer gilds them yet,
But all, except their Sun, is set.

Byron, *Don Juan,* Canto 3

In his acceptance speech in New York City, following his election
as PEN president in 1979, Bernard Malamud commented on his new
location: "I live most of the year miles away, in a small town in
Vermont, where I write full-time and teach in the spring."[1] He has
ceased to be an active walker in the city like Alfred Kazin. His
peripatetic efforts would now seem devoted to the New England
countryside much like the hero of his most recent novel, William B.
Dubin. New England, for Malamud and an entire generation of New
York Jews, used to be the setting for summer camps and other warm-
weather retreats to escape the punishing and debilitating heat of the
city. It was a forbidding land, dominated by Boston Brahmins and
wild-eyed Calvinists, suitable for month-long vacations but not for
permanent living.

The situation has changed. Malamud's move to Vermont and his
teaching commitment at Bennington College seem part of a pattern.
Stanley Edgar Hyman, another Jew from New York, also taught at
Bennington. Joining him in this Vermont setting was the Californian
Shirley Jackson, who married Hyman in 1940 after their graduation
from Syracuse and settled in to write her elegant fiction—like that
haunting *New Yorker* story "The Lottery" and her classic short novel
We Have Always Lived in the Castle—with its unmistakable New

England textures. Both died in early middle age: she in 1965, he in 1970. Another New England writing couple is Robert Penn Warren and Eleanor Clark—the marriage of a Kentucky-born Agrarian, who finished his academic career at Yale, with a long-time resident of Connecticut.

The roster keeps swelling all the time, as outsiders continue to join native sons and daughters. New England has become a kind of *umbilicus mundi* as it has reached out to welcome the Soviet exile, Alexander Solzhenitsyn, the only woman writer ever to be elected to the French Academy, the Belgian-born Marguerite Yourcenar, as well as talented writers from other parts of the country, like William Styron, John Updike, J.D. Salinger, Philip Roth, Peter De Vries, and Norman Mailer. When one adds to the list native New Englanders like John Hawkes and John Cheever, one begins to imagine another renaissance such as the one that New England had in the mid-nineteenth century or that the American South had during the age of the Fugitives which coincided nicely with the first decade of Faulkner's publishing life.

Alas, this is not the case. The five-year period (1850–1855) which F.O. Matthiessen devoted so much attention to in his *American Renaissance* and the equally remarkable period in Southern literature eighty years later have no equivalent in New England fiction writing since 1950. This gathering of so much talent in Connecticut and Massachusetts, particularly, but also in Vermont, New Hampshire, Maine, and Rhode Island, has left no indelible stamp on our literary consciousness. Indeed the best of the writers I have mentioned thus far either do not write about New England at all or else permit it only grudging passageway through the back door of their fiction.

While Eleanor Clark dutifully tills the literary soil of Vermont in her latest novel, *Gloria Mundi*, her husband, Robert Penn Warren, keeps returning to his Kentucky roots. Witness his most recent novel, *A Place to Come To*, or his splendid long piece in *The New Yorker* (February 25, 1980) on Jefferson Davis, which starts by recalling Warren's own youth in Guthrie, Kentucky: "I am a small boy sitting tailor-fashion on the unkempt lawn, looking up at the old man, and then, beyond him, at the whitewashed board fence, and then at the woods coming down almost to the fence. If it was getting toward sunset, the uncountable guinea fowl would be coming in from foraging to roost near the house, making a metallic and disgruntled but halfhearted clatter, not the full, outraged racket of morning" (p. 44). This is as elegant a description of place as his wife offers of Boonton, Vermont, in *Gloria Mundi*, but it is clearly a different one.

John Hawkes has lived virtually all of his life in New England—born in Stamford, Connecticut, educated at Harvard, and a member of the Brown faculty since 1958—but has consistently avoided his native region in choosing his "lunar landscapes" (Leslie Fiedler's happy expression, used by Hawkes as the title of his 1969 collection of short fiction). His intentionally hazy settings, Germany in *The Cannibal*, Italy in "The Owl" and "The Goose on the Grave," the American West in *The Beetle Leg*, England in *The Lime Twig*, and the South of France in *Travesty*, are not only far removed geographically from the northeastern states which have always been his home but also temperamentally, poetically, and even morally. The closest he seems to get to the irregular coast of New England is "the gentle island" Skipper and Cassandra briefly inhabit in *Second Skin*.

William Styron, a long-time resident of Roxbury, Connecticut, is usually drawn to his native Virginia for his literary settings. He has detoured on several occasions but mainly to European backdrops. In his latest novel, *Sophie's Choice*, he uses Flatbush as the still point which anchors a restless narrative which moves easily through historical and fictional time. Flatbush, however, is still a long subway ride from Connecticut and the Merritt Parkway, that gateway to New England.[2] And Styron's Brooklyn, which he refers to as "the Kingdom of the Jews," is especially far away from the cool, aloof Protestant world to the north.

Norman Mailer now gives as his address Provincetown, Massachusetts, but the settings of his special brand of nonfiction novel are determined by the dictates and emphases of journalists, not by his current surroundings. Mailer seems more wedded to the caprices of newspaper reporters than to those of his own imagination. Thus his most recent book, the Pulitzer Prize–winning *The Executioner's Song* (called a "true life novel" on the dustjacket), devotes itself to the much publicized Gary Gilmore's death-by-firing-squad in Utah.

I seem to have skimmed off much of the cream already, by eliminating Warren, Hawkes, Styron, and Mailer. Updike is certainly tuned into the cadences and vagaries of New England life in *Couples* and *Marry Me*, but he reverts to the more familiar rhythms of Pennsylvania in his best fiction, like *Rabbit, Run, Rabbit Redux*, and

The Centaur. Salinger has been silent for so many years (as have his campus admirers) that he is no longer a vital force of any kind. Even when he was writing his cult literature, New York was the central presence, rarely New England.

All of which is to say that the physical presence in New England of all these talented writers should not make us think that these northeasternmost states are undergoing another (what Matthiessen called) "extraordinarily concentrated moment of expression." These gifted contemporaries are looking in too many directions—invariably away from New England rather than toward it—for there to be any talk of another "flowering" or "rebirth." Indeed if Van Wyck Brooks were still alive and had in mind a sequel to his *The Flowering of New England* and *New England: Indian Summer*, that most euphoric of critics might have been forced to come up with an unencouraging title like *The Deflowering of New England* or, with a nod to Tennyson and Huxley, *After Many a Summer Dies the Swan.* There are of course many New England writers and much New England fiction. But renaissances are not fashioned by novels like *Love Story*, *Oliver's Story*, and *Man, Woman and Child.*

Perhaps the most hopeful recent development was the appearance in 1979 of first-rate fiction by Malamud and Roth, two of those neophyte New Englanders. Malamud's *Dubin's Lives* and Roth's *The Ghost Writer* are indeed the first example of New England fiction written by either.

Dubin's Lives is set "in New York State, almost a mile from the Vermont border."[3] William Dubin's long walks, which grow longer as his biographical labors grow more frustrating, often take him across the border. Dubin's New England credentials are, in fact, impeccable despite his origins in "Newark and Bronx tenements." He is the author of a biography of Thoreau, that "woodsy dybbuk," and had flirted with the possibility of a life of Robert Frost only to be rejected by that poet who "had already chosen someone 'to preserve my immortal remains' " (p. 12).

Dubin's Lives takes the Jewish biographer, with the ex-Episcopalian wife and the 22-year-old mistress who alternates between the wearing of the Star of David and the Cross of Jesus, to points as distant as Venice and Stockholm. But the still point which anchors his biographical activities is the New England countryside. Dubin, the urban Jew who seems to have deserted the city as well as his religion, considers himself a "visitor to nature." Yet he feels increasingly in tune with its rhythms and vibrations:

> Dubin, after a decade and a half in Center Campobello, could recognize and name about twenty trees, a half dozen bushes, fifteen wild flowers, a handful of birds. He followed the flight of a crow elated to know who was flying. He had slowly learned to look, name things of nature. When he passed a flower he told himself to take it all in (p. 9).

Malamud himself probably had some of the same adjusting to do when he first came to Bennington, but he had the advantage of arriving from another rural setting, Corvallis, Oregon.

The "outsider" William B. Dubin comes to terms with his various displacements. He warms increasingly to his latest biographical effort, the fleshing out of the life of D. H. Lawrence. His relationship with his mistress Fanny (named after Jane Austen's Fanny Price) seemed built on a series of still-born literary allusions; the ups and downs of his liaison precisely mirrored the details of Lawrence's irregular existence with Frieda. Dubin, in fact, was almost aware that he was making life imitate his biographical art as he played Lawrence to Fanny's Frieda. By the end of the novel, however, he appears to have resolved his personal as well as his creative problems: Fanny leaves to pursue a career in law; Dubin has worked things out with his wife; the final page of *Dubin's Lives* lists among the "Works by William B. Dubin" *The Passion of D. H. Lawrence: A Life*, indicating that he has triumphed over his biographer's block and properly separated life from art. And all of this was managed in the New England countryside, which has become a surrogate home for this diaspora urban Jew.

Philip Roth's *The Ghost Writer*, as several reviewers have suggested, bears an uncommon likeness to *Dubin's Lives*. Roth is another of these intruders on the New England soil just as the 56-year-old writer E. I. Lonoff is. *The Ghost Writer* is Lonoff's story as filtered through the active imagination of Roth's narrator, Nathan Zuckerman (a character on loan from an earlier novel, *My Life as a Man*). The New England countryside is once again on display: Lonoff's "clapboard farmhouse was at the end of an unpaved road twelve hundred feet up in the Berkshires. . . ."[4] But this writer, once referred to by Zuckerman as "the region's most original storyteller since Melville and Hawthorne" (p. 4), seems less comfortable with

his surroundings than William Dubin. When his wife, Hope, a
member of an establishment New England family, insists that her
Jewish husband needs more exercise, he responds: "I can't face
another walk. I can't face those trees again.... For ten years I walked
in the other direction. That's why I started walking in this direction.
Besides, I'm not even walking when I'm walking. The truth is, I don't
even see the trees" (p. 158). He denies "the walk" the grandeur and
poetry that Proust's narrator attached to it when he spoke of the "two
'ways' which we used to take for our walks, and so diametrically
opposed that we would actually leave the house by a different door,
according to the way we had chosen: the way towards Méséglise-la-
Vineuse, which we called also 'Swann's way,' because, to get there,
one had to pass along the boundary of M. Swann's estate, and the
'Guermantes way.' "[5]

The reference to Proust here serves an additional purpose. Proust
was part of that modernist generation which made the plight of the
artist a central concern of their fiction. Along with Mann, Joyce, and
James (all of whom are at least mentioned in *The Ghost Writer*), he
made the type of the writer an expected ingredient in the literary works
of the better part of a half century. Henry James seemed to start it all
in the 1880s and 1890s with that succession of artist stories, one of
which, "The Middle Years," is a crucial presence in Roth's latest
book. Indeed three sentences from this story appear on a bulletin
board near Lonoff's writing table, including the famous "The rest is
the madness of art." Zuckerman puzzles over these words and finally
reads the story twice. "The Middle Years" is obviously a central text
for *The Ghost Writer* as it illumines the various relationships in
Roth's novelette. The three central characters are all artists of sorts:
Zuckerman, the author of four stories, who seeks to apprentice
himself to the "master" E. I. Lonoff; Amy Bellette,[6] who has already
passed through a Lonoff apprenticeship and, through a systematic
myth Zuckerman "had evolved about her" (p. 157), has been
metamorphosed into the author of *The Diary of Anne Frank*.

Not only is the James story of crucial importance but also James
himself, he who spent formative years in New England and returned
many years later to record in *The American Scene* this convoluted
sentence: "That *is* Arcadia in fact, and questions drop, or at least get
themselves deferred and shiftlessly shirked; in conformity with which
truth the New England hills and woods—since they were not all, for

the weeks to come, of mere New Hampshire—the mild September glow and even the clear October blaze were things to play on the chords of memory and association, to say nothing of those of surprise, with an admirable art of their own."[7] James's "New England hills and woods" prove appealing to Zuckerman, who is in retreat from his Newark boyhood. Lonoff balks a little, though he has himself lived in New England from the age of seven, when "he was shipped alone from Jaffa to wealthy relatives of his father's in Brookline" (p. 32), and now seems curiously devoted to "those black Massachusetts hills" (pp. 27–28). Amy Bellette moves with ease between Cambridge, where she works in the Harvard library, and the Lonoff household—with the excuse that she means to sort through the celebrated writer's manuscripts so they can eventually be turned over to Harvard. She seems almost as committed to New England as she is to Lonoff and his work.

Dubin's Lives and *The Ghost Writer* are novels about Jews who have found refuge of a sort in rural New England (just as Moses Herzog did before them). Malamud and Roth have not so much shifted subject as scene. They have both moved their familiar literary baggage to a new setting and have written some of the best fiction to come out of this region in a long time.

Leslie Fiedler, in his justly famous "The Jew in the American Novel," uncovers Jewish characters as far back in American literature as Charles Brockden Brown's *Arthur Mervyn* (1799). He notes that the earliest are stereotyped women, nurtured on the prejudices of the Anglo-Saxon majority. When a distinct Jewish-American literature came into being in the 1930s little help was offered by previous Jewish appearances in fiction. The New England soil has seemed especially unreceptive to the growth of a Jewish fiction. Jews have been known to gather in large urban centers and New England has but one of these, Boston. Boston has indeed been the setting for much of the Polonsky saga of Charles Angoff, beginning with *Journey to the Dawn* (1951). The second novel in the sequence, *In the Morning Light* (1952), takes place almost entirely in Boston and chronicles, in an interesting sociological way, the coming of age of David Polonsky (Angoff's fictional representative). The author kept adding to the saga—there are eleven novels in all—until his death in May, 1979. Angoff's novel-sequence may be said, in certain ways, to be the Boston-Jewish equivalent of those New York-Jewish novels of the

1930s, Henry Roth's *Call It Sleep* and Daniel Fuchs' Williamsburg trilogy. But the comparison ends abruptly when one begins to apply literary standards, as Angoff's fictional talents fail completely to measure up to those of Roth and Fuchs.

There is really no such thing as a Boston Jewish novel, despite the valiant efforts of Charles Angoff, although *Dubin's Lives* and *The Ghost Writer* urge upon us the possibility of a New England Jewish novel in the future. At the moment, however, as we survey the scene since 1950, we find the increasing presence of Jewish characters in New England novels, rarely playing the lead role but usually functioning somewhere in the wings. They are sometimes treated as pariahs and cast in stereotypical moulds, but writers as different as John Updike, Eleanor Clark, Theodore Morrison, May Sarton, and Sloan Wilson have tried to relieve them of these clichéd formulas. The Jew is no longer quite the embarrassing presence he was to the Hawthorne of *The Marble Faun*.

John Updike is the most intriguing case of all. His fascination with the Jew and Jewish subjects is evident in *Bech: A Book*, which chronicles the world travels and adventures of the novelist Henry Bech, who admits that "his favorite Jewish writer was the one who turned his back on his three beautiful Brooklyn novels and went into the desert to write scripts for Doris Day." (Any devotee of the Jewish American novel will recognize Daniel Fuchs in this description.) Updike seems never to tire of the indefatigable Bech who keeps turning up in *New Yorker* and *Playboy* stories, indeed as recently as the December, 1979 *Playboy*. Bech, whimsically described in these later stories as "the exquisitely unprolific author," "the scarcely read yet oddly respectable American author," the recipient of "the Melville Medal, awarded every five years to that American author who has maintained the most meaningful silence," touches down almost everywhere in his travels. Although Updike's satirical edge is probably never quite so sharp as in the ongoing Bech saga, Bech himself emerges as a compellingly fleshed-out portrait of the wandering Jewish artist.

Perhaps before the portrait is completed Henry Bech will have a genuine New England interlude, more substantial than the annual rental of a cottage on a Massachusetts island. For the moment one has to turn to *Couples* for a view of Jews—a rather oblique one at that—residing in New England. The setting of this novel, Tarbox, Massachusetts, accommodates a variety of adulterous couples who indulge in more than their share of spouse swapping. Updike seems to have made an effort to include as many national and religious types as possible, thus suggesting a world in miniature. Living among the Congregationalists, Episcopalians, Presbyterians, and Catholics are the Saltzes, who seem ill-suited to the way of life prescribed by Tarbox and are never quite accepted by its establishment. Ben and Irene Saltz who, fittingly, are always on the periphery, are given only passing attention by Updike. They are never quite on the cutting edge of things, but that seems very much to their credit in this environment which nurtures pretense, infidelity, and a general sense of malaise. At one point toward the end of the novel, just before their departure from Tarbox, the Saltzes invite Piet Hanema (the principal character in the novel, if there is one) to dinner. In a gesture of genuine affection, Ben tries to cheer up the husband who now lives alone in a "shabby room": " 'You're down now,' he told Piet, 'and it's a pity you're not a Jew, because the fact is, every Jew expects to be down sometime in his life, and he has a philosophy for it. God is testing him. *Nisay on Elohim.*' "[8] Piet's Calvinism should probably have equipped him for this encounter, but it sadly did not; he is none the wiser when he leaves the Saltzes.

Ben's Hebrew, with its rhythms of authenticity, punctuates his conversation. It is curiously out of joint with the Princeton-learned French of another character, Harold little-Smith, which phonily and ungrammatically speaks for the WASP society of Tarbox. Harold's mistress Janet boasts early in the novel of "our lovely churches and old houses and marshes and absolutely grand beach. I think we're the prettiest unselfconscious town in America." This follows the far more revealing comment about Tarbox: "Like everything in New England, it's passé, only more so" (p. 36). As if in proof of the latter statement, the Congregational Church, attended by Piet Hanema, burns down toward the end of the novel. This perhaps has something in common with those fires at the end of *The Spoils of Poynton* and *Absalom, Absalom!* It sounds the conclusion of a way of life just as those other more dramatic fires in James and Faulkner did. Piet's "Calvinist God," whom he refers to so frequently, asserts His wrath. The Saltzes alone seem to be beyond His reach; they have left Tarbox and "sent cards to everyone at Christmas" (p. 478).[9]

Eleanor Clark's *Gloria Mundi*, which shifts the scene to Vermont, also offers a Calvinistic landscape: "It's original sin, I suppose, with whatever frills you pick up from your life,"[10] as one of the characters remarks. The prose itself has something of a Calvinistic bleakness, almost as if it were filtered through a succession of "dark" books like Melville's *Pierre*, Faulkner's *Light in August*, and Gass's *Omensetter's Luck*.

Lem Palz is the unlikely Jewish presence in this setting. He and his wife, Hannah, have become a kind of moral center for the town of Boonton, Vermont. The townspeople look upon this couple (he Jewish, she not, despite her Old Testament name) as attractive eccentrics who have brought special warmth and vitality to the Vermont village where they have lived "for almost thirty years" (p. 24). Despite their longtime presence in Boonton there remains something of the "outsider" about both of them: she was a Trotskyite at one time and he was hunted by the Nazis in France during World War II. F. D. Reeve describes them accurately in a recent review of *Gloria Mundi*: "Living well is chiefly the assignment of the erudite, sensitive, idealistic and sophisticated Palzes, Hannah and Lem, characters of refinement themselves, witnesses to others' character."[11] It is in their roles as witness and proprietor of "their little Green Mt.Taliesin" (p. 25) that they serve a community which seems almost to require their graciousness and hospitality to survive. They are a stabilizing force in Eleanor Clark's uncertain world of runaway clergymen, runaway midwesterners, and runaway teenage girls. Hannah reminds one somewhat of William Dubin when we are told: "She often hiked miles in the woods, on the lookout for a new patch of chanterelles or an unusual variety of fern or ladyslipper . . ." (p. 23). The Jewish Lem and his wife, Hannah, who sometimes despairs "that I'm not a Jew too" (p. 71), seem more essential to *Gloria Mundi* than Jewish characters are to most of the other novels under discussion. Yet, predictably, they never quite have the importance of Margo Philipson, the daughter of a Methodist minister and wife of an Episcopalian minister, or that Episcopalian minister himself, John Philipson. New England is still emphatically Protestant country.

And so it is in Theodore Morrison's *The Stones of the House*, the setting of which is Rowley University, with its "Episcopalian past." This is another of the species of academic novel which proliferated during the 1940s, 1950s,and 1960s—often the handiwork of career professors like Morrison himself, who taught English at Harvard for many years.[12] *The Stones of the House* begins with the acting president, Andrew Aiken, discussing a disturbed Jewish philosophy professor, Maurice Holsberg, with the college chaplain, Martin Holmes. The set of circumstances and the names are predictable as is the direction of Aiken's remarks: " 'It isn't so much the size of the place, though, that matters to Maurice; it's the milieu. He really ought to be an urban character, I suppose, a real cosmopolite. He needs theaters, art galleries, concerts, a Bohemia where people talk nonsense about art and society but at least keep ideas in a state of agitation. A city of a couple of hundred thousand, like ours, mainly the result of mushrooming industry, doesn't give Maurice the food his system needs.' "[13] Almost all of the clichés about Jews and their special needs are present in these well-intentioned comments. Indeed Aiken devotes much selfless attention to Holsberg's psychological problems during an especially trying period in the life of the university and of himself. He manages to get the philosophy professor released from teaching for a short period during the semester and arranges for a sabbatical for him. He even puts up Holsberg's father at his house and discusses his son's problems with him. The elder Holsberg at this point offers a set piece on the Jews, which is composed of an embarrassing series of platitudes: "In the middle ages, we Jews were despised as usurers. We were among the pioneers of capitalism when it was feared and hated as a mysterious revolution. Now we're suspected of international communism, disloyalty to the states who so cheerfully and patriotically destroy each other. When it comes to that, we're suspected of both crimes at once" (p. 168). These remarks continue in the same vein, punctuated with clichéd turns like "God's elect tribe," "covenant of earthly and heavenly promise," "the Jew his unique role of scapegoat," "that distinctively Jewish phenomenon, self-hatred." If Theodore Morrison's intention were to ridicule the elder Holsberg, one might understand this gathering of tired-out ethnic phrasing. But that, alas, is clearly not the case.

Perhaps we can say that *The Stones of the House* is the kind of novel people expected and responded to in the naive, undaring 1950s. Minorities were to be delivered over in stereotyped formulas, solutions were to be tidy and irrevocable. Thus, by the end of the book, Andrew Aiken gets the presidency of Rowley, the wealthy alumnus commits his money to build a new library, Aiken's daughter is about to marry the ideal young man. Aiken's interest in Maurice

Holsberg's career seems to have paid off in handsome dividends, almost as if some divine New England providence were at work.

A far more sophisticated novel of this period, with some of the same vibrations, is May Sarton's *Faithful are the Wounds.* It is well known that this is a *roman à clef:* the suicide of Edward Cavan is a literary rendering of the suicide of F. O. Matthiessen. People familiar with the Harvard scene at midcentury—Theodore Morrison, for example—would probably be able to offer additional keys to the identities of the other characters. We get glimpses of Cavan, his friends, his colleagues, his sister, and a favorite graduate student. The backdrop of the Henry Wallace campaign informs most of the novel; the epilogue, which occurs five years later, is seasoned by the McCarthy hearings. In the midst of this political ambience is the seemingly apolitical Jewish professor, Ivan Goldberg. The first view of him is rather forbidding: "This was a face that never relaxed, was never to be caught off guard. . . . Goldberg had contrived a façade which no one had ever seen through completely. . . . He had made it his business to have all the answers within his field of English and American literature, and he did not range outside it. Absolutely concentrated, with a mind like a fencer's, he was bound to win."[14] The Jew as liberal and espouser of lost causes is nowhere evident in this portrait. Just before his suicide Edward appeals to Goldberg to head a Harvard committee to protest the firing of a professor in another university who campaigned for Wallace or at least to sign a petition in his behalf. Goldberg roundly refuses him: " 'We don't do things that way at Harvard, as you know very well. . . . No, Edward, I have steadfastly refused to be involved in political matters and I don't see why I should suddenly go back on my position now' " (p. 106).

Ivan Goldberg's "ivory tower" position (as Edward calls it) is interestingly dealt with by May Sarton. Before *Faithful are the Wounds* has ended, Goldberg has partly ventured outside of this ivory tower. When Edward's sister arrives in Cambridge for the funeral, she lunches with Goldberg. He emerges from this encounter far more sympathetically than from the earlier one with Edward. We see him shortly after during the funeral service: "Goldberg never entered a Christian church without feeling himself drawn down into a whirlpool of anguish of different kinds. For him the word 'Jesus Christ' was a terrible word. He could not bear it without remembering centuries of pogroms, his father's stories of their grandfather's village in Russia and the terrors of Easter when the Christians went forth to kill any Jews not locked up in their houses, the doors double barred and their hearts like animal hearts feeling only the fear of the hunted" (p. 217). This is a far more genuine and compelling view of the Jew's dilemma than the one offered by Holsberg *père* in *The Stones of the House.* May Sarton knows something that Theodore Morrison did not. Goldberg's *Menschheit* seems completed when we discover at the end of the novel that he has dedicated his latest book to Edward Cavan and has "stood up lately and spoken out" (p. 265).

Theodore Morrison went on to write an unfortunate sequel to *The Stones of the House* with another very solemn title, *To Make a World.* May Sarton shifted to a small girls' college in New England, with "an atmosphere rather different from laissez-faire sophisticated Harvard's" in *The Small Room.*

A Calvinistic loneliness pervades *The Small Room* as it does another novel with a New England academic backdrop, Louis Auchincloss' *The Rector of Justin.* This book, set in an Episcopal boys' boarding school not far from Boston, chronicles through a series of perspectives—mostly in the form of diary jottings, memoirs, and notes, but very coherently managed—the life of the founder and headmaster, Francis Prescott. The headmaster's wife is a great-niece of Emerson and virtually everyone in the novel has impeccable New England credentials. This is an ordered, decorous society in which the best literature and art are politely discussed. For example, early in the novel there is a discussion about James's *Ambassadors* which has the hollow ring of safe, establishment literary criticism. The use of *The Ambassadors* here is radically different from Roth's use of "The Middle Years" in *The Ghost Writer.*

Jews apparently have no place in Justin Martyr, this "Protestant school for boys of Anglo-Saxon descent." There are, however, occasional references to them in *The Rector of Justin.* Francis Prescott seems to have no objection to Jews attending his prestigious prep school as long as they are willing "to attend every chapel service and every sacred studies class!" He uses the word *Christian* to embrace all men of good will, even Jews: " 'I have never admitted the word "Jew" as any but a religious term.' "[15] This graduate of Balliol, during the time Jowett was Master of the college, seems never to have emerged from the century of Disraeli, he who had, according to Lionel Stevenson, along with "his pride in his Jewish forebears" a "belief that Christianity was the fulfillment of Hebraism."[16]

Unlike the somewhat fossilized Prescott, the typical Sloan Wilson protagonist, although he is acutely aware of his Puritan ancestry, of his New England background, tries desperately to "live in the present." Wilson's characters have the same respect for the establishment eastern seaboard families, with their prep school and Harvard-Yale backgrounds, as do Auchincloss'. (Wilson has a Harvard degree, Auchincloss one from Yale.) Yet Wilson's seem to struggle more with a world which holds on to the old pieties and stubbornly resists change.

The central work in Wilson's canon is *The Man in the Gray Flannel Suit,* which is set in Connecticut, first in Westport, then in South Bay. Tom Rath is one of those post-World War II commuters who shuttle back and forth between their place of work, New York City, and their homes. This Harvard graduate is very concerned with what we now call "upward mobility" as he changes jobs early in the novel. A series of things occur which make his life-style increasingly ragged and hectic, including the reminder of a wartime love affair he had with an Italian girl, Maria. Rath's honesty wins out at the end of the novel as he reveals the affair to his wife and arranges to send money to Maria on a regular basis to help bring up their illegitimate child. Then, significantly, Tom Rath and his wife leave for a week-long vacation in Vermont, a place with considerably purer air.

Toward the middle of the novel, after the Raths have moved to South Bay, they attend *en famille* the local Episcopal church. That Sunday afternoon Tom first hears of a Jewish probate judge, Saul Bernstein, who becomes a kind of catalytic presence through the rest of *The Man in the Gray Flannel Suit.* Bernstein's background involves the usual heady dose of anti-Semitism. Early in his career he was told "that he ought to go into New York to practice law, because there was no place for a Jewish attorney in a small, hidebound Connecticut town notorious for its prejudice against Jews."[17] Yet he stayed on in South Bay, with its old Episcopal families, and gained prominence on the Probate Court even though he was never quite accepted socially. His honesty is one of the vital forces in the novel as it outlasts the pretense and hypocrisy of the rest of the community. It is fitting that the final paragraph of the novel should be turned over to him in his role as chorus and moral conscience. This Jew who derives pleasure and strength from helping to restore balance has become a more familiar figure in the New England novel. But nowhere is he more sympathetically drawn than in the character of Saul Bernstein. The emphasis in this essay has been much more on outsiders than on insiders. Some of the most talented writers in the country have chosen to live in New England—often moving there from distant points—without writing about it. Oddly enough, the best recent fiction seems to have come from two urban Jewish novelists who have decided only in their latest books to write about rural New England. Increasingly Jewish characters, interlopers, have become dynamic presences in the novels of a region long dominated by Congregationalists and Episcopalians. These are some of the curiosities we have looked at.

But something of an older New England, perhaps a more eccentric and untouched New England, is found in the remarkable fiction of John Cheever. One need only turn to *The Wapshot Chronicle* and *The Wapshot Scandal,* with their setting in St. Botolphs, Massachusetts, which "was an old place, an old river town,"[18] to uncover some of these special effects. Cheever would probably have nothing to do with my notion of a deflowering of New England. He comments knowingly in *The Wapshot Scandal:* "It is late in the day, late in this history of this part of the world, but this lateness does nothing to eclipse their ardor."[19] The ardor is certainly present in Cheever's fiction but sadly missing almost everywhere else.

NOTES

1. Bernard Malamud, "A Fellowship of Writers," *PEN American Center Newsletter,* No. 41 (September, 1979), p. 1.

2. There is an amusing conversation about it in J. D. Salinger's "Uncle Wiggily in Connecticut": "She [Mary Jane] explained to Eloise, who had come out to the driveway to meet her, that everything had been absolutely *perfect*, that she had remembered the way *exactly*, until she had turned off the Merrick Parkway. Eloise said, '*Merritt* Parkway, baby.' . . ." This passage is found in *Nine Stories* (New York: Signet, 1960), p. 18.

3. Bernard Malamud, *Dubin's Lives* (New York: Farrar, Straus & Giroux, 1979), p. 13. All subsequent references will be to this edition.

4. Philip Roth, *The Ghost Writer* (New York: Farrar, Straus & Giroux, 1979), p. 3. All subsequent references will be to this edition.

5. Marcel Proust, *Swann's Way*, trans. C. K. Scott Moncrieff (New York: Modern Library, 1956), p. 191.

6. Mark Krupnick offers an ingenious explanation for the choice of this name, which sounds like "aimer belles-lettres." See his "The Middle Years," *Inquiry* (October 15, 1979), p. 22.

7. Henry James, *The American Scene*, "Introduction" by Irving Howe (New York: Horizon Press, 1967), pp. 13–14.

8. John Updike, *Couples* (Greenwich: Fawcett, 1969), pp. 439–40. All subsequent references will be to this edition.

9. Updike's *Marry Me* is another New England novel about "couples"; this time he concentrates on only two. The Lutheran and Unitarian churches are central presences. Judaism is not mentioned.

10. Eleanor Clark, *Gloria Mundi* (New York: Pantheon Books, 1979), p. 70. All subsequent references will be to this edition. Another noteworthy recent Vermont novel is John Gardner's *October Light* (1976).

11. See *New England Review*, 2 (Winter, 1979), 271.

12. For a good discussion of the academic novel, see John O. Lyons, *The College Novel in America* (Carbondale: Southern Illinois Univ. Press, 1962).

13. Theodore Morrison, *The Stones of the House* (New York: Viking, 1953), p. 5. All subsequent references will be to this edition.

14. May Sarton, *Faithful are the Wounds* (New York: Rinehart & Company, 1955), pp. 103–04. All subsequent references will be to this edition.

15. Louis Auchincloss, *The Rector of Justin* (Boston: Houghton Mifflin, 1964), p. 297.

16. Lionel Stevenson, *The English Novel: A Panorama* (Boston: Houghton Mifflin, 1960), p. 256.

17. Sloan Wilson, *The Man in the Gray Flannel Suit* (New York: Pocket Books, 1964), p. 137.

18. John Cheever, *The Wapshot Chronicle* (New York: Harper & Brothers, 1957), p. 3. When I read Cheever's Wapshot novels I am reminded of a remark made by Austin Warren in his *The New England Conscience* (Ann Arbor: Univ. of Michigan Press, 1966), p. 209: "New England has long been rich in eccentrics; and the New England village of my youth could manage a considerable number."

19. John Cheever, *The Wapshot Scandal* (New York: Harper & Row, 1964), p. 21.

Index

Abolition, theme of, in
   Uncle Tom's Cabin, 107
Abolitionists, relationship of, to
   Federalists, 39
Absalom! Absalom! (Faulkner),
   mentioned, 175
"Acquainted with the Night"
   (Frost), difference of,
   from Emerson, 132
Acrostics, seventeenth-century
   poets' attraction to, 13–14
African-American Repository, 91
African Benevolent Society,
   proceedings and corre-
   spondence of, 85
"After Apple-Picking" (Frost),
   139–40, 141
Alhambra, The (Jones), 125
Alienation
   of Federalist writers, 39
   of female artist, 163–64
   male artists and, 163
   of Plath, 154, 155, 157
   of Sexton, 157
Allen, Ethan, as subject of
   Triumph of Infidelity, The
   (Dwight), 33
Allston, Washington, 35
"America! America!" (Plath),
   155–56
America and Other Poems
   (Whitefield), 91

"American, An" (Kipling),
   admiration of, by Howells,
   114
American Colonization Society,
   mentioned, 90
"American Scholar, The"
   (Emerson), 53
Ames, Fisher, similarity of, with
   Thoreau, 39–40
Amy Bellette (*The Ghost Writer*),
   significance of name of,
   172, 173, 182 n.6
Anagrams, seventeenth-century
   poets' attraction to, 13–15
Anarchiad, The (Barlow)
   as apocalypticism, 45
   mentioned, 32
Andrew Aiken (*The Stones of the
   House*), 177–78
Angoff, Charles
   In the Morning Light, 173
   Journey to the Dawn, 173
   Polansky saga of, 173
Antebellum period. *See* Early
   national period
Antifederalism. *See* Federalism,
   bias against
Apocalypticism in the early
   national period, 45
Appeal, in Four Articles . . .
   (Walker), 93–94
Ariel (Plath), 154

trilogy of, 174
Fugitive Slave Law, Daniel
  Webster as defender of, 107
Fuller, Margaret, as feminist,
  mentioned, 107
Funeral elegy, satires of, 17–19
"Fuzzy Wuzzy" (Kipling), as
  blues, 118

Gardner, John, *October Light,*
  182 n. 10
Gass, William, *Omensetter's
  Luck,* mentioned, 176
"Georgie Porgie" (Kipling),
  imperialism in, mentioned,
  119
"Getting There" (Plath), 158
Ghost Writer, The (Philip Roth),
  170, 171–72
  likeness of, to *Dubin's Lives,*
    171
  New England setting of, 171
  significance of *The American
    Scene* to, 172–73
  significance of "The Middle
    Years" to, 172
  style of, compared to Proust,
    172
"Gift Outright, The" (Frost),
  influence of Emerson on,
  137
Gilbert, Claudius, subject of
  anagram, 15
Gilbert, Sandra M., and Susan
  Gubar, *Madwoman in the
  Attic,* 147
Ginsberg, Allen, mentioned, 45
Gloria Mundi (Clark), 175–76
  review of, by Reeve, 176
  setting of, 168, 169
"Goose on the Grave, The"
  (Hawkes), setting of, 169
Gospelmanna (Dunster), 13–14
"Grammarians Funeral, The"
  (Tompson), 18–19

Grandy, Moses, *Narrative,* 86
"Green Eyes of the Little Yellow
  God, The" (Kipling), as
  blues, mentioned, 122
Greenfield Hill (Dwight)
  preromantic elements in, 38
  as romantic writing, 32
Grimke, Angelina Weld, 82–83
  Rachel, 82–83
Gubar, Susan, and Sandra M.
  Gilbert, *Madwoman in the
  Attic,* 147
Guilt
  of slavery, New Englanders',
    107–10
  of Stowe, 110–11, 112
  as theme in Sexton's poems,
    151–52
"Gunga Din" (Kipling), as blues,
  118

Hall, Prince, *Charge Delivered
  to the Brethren of the
  African Lodge, on the
  Twenty-Fifth of June, 1792,
  in Charlestown,* 87–88
Halleck, Fitz-Greene, mentioned,
  35
Hammon, Briton, mentioned, 92
Handy, W.C., on the blues,
  116–17
Hannah Palz *(Gloria Mundi),* 176
"Happiness Makes Up in Height
  What It Lacks in Length"
  (Frost), 138–39
"Hardship of Accounting, The"
  (Frost), similarities of, with
  Emerson's "Wealth," 137
Harlem Renaissance, mentioned,
  82
Harold little-Smith *(Couples),* 175
Harris, Sheldon (publisher of
  black letters), 84
Harte, Bret, influence of, on
  Kipling, mentioned, 114